A WORD A DAY

GRADE 2

Editorial Development: Marilyn Evans
Robyn Raymer
Sarita Chávez
Silverman
Susan Rose Simms
Copy Editing: Carrie Gwynne
Art Direction: Cheryl Puckett
Cover Design: David Price
Design/Production: Susan Bigger
John D. Williams

EMC 2792

Evan-Moor®
EDUCATIONAL PUBLISHERS
Helping Children Learn since 1979

Congratulations on your purchase of some of the finest teaching materials in the world.

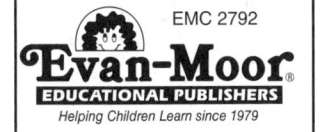

Photocopying the pages in this book is permitted for single-classroom use only. Making photocopies for additional classes or schools is prohibited.

For information about other Evan-Moor products, call 1-800-777-4362, fax 1-800-777-4332, or visit our Web site, www.evan-moor.com. Entire contents © 2009 EVAN-MOOR CORP. 18 Lower Ragsdale Drive, Monterey, CA 93940-5746. Printed in USA.

Correlated to State Standards
Visit *teaching-standards.com* to view a correlation of this book's activities to your state's standards. This is a free service.

Weekly Walk-Through

Each week of **A Word a Day** follows the same format, making it easy for both students and teacher to use.

Words of the Week

Four new words are presented each week. A definition, example sentence, and discussion prompts are provided for each word.

Part of Speech The part of speech is identified. You may or may not want to share this information with the class, depending on the skill level of your students.

Example Sentence Each new word is used in a sentence designed to provide enough context for students to easily grasp its meaning. The same sentence is found in the reproducible student dictionary, which begins on page 148.

Critical Attributes Prompt Discussion questions are provided that require students to identify features that are and are not attributes of the target word. This is one of the most effective ways to help students recognize subtleties of meaning.

Definition Each word is defined in a complete sentence. The same definition is found in the reproducible student dictionary, which begins on page 148.

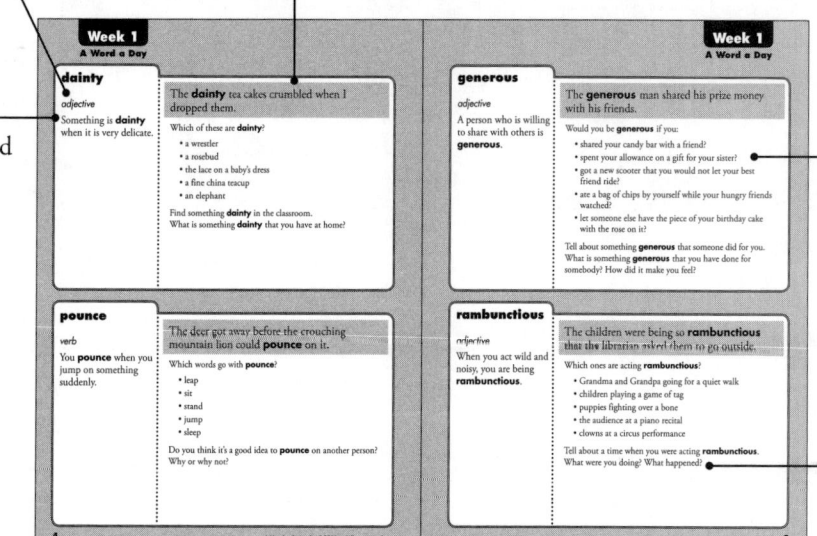

Personal Connection Prompt Students are asked to share an opinion, an idea, or a personal experience that demonstrates their understanding of the new word.

How to Present the Words

Use one of the following methods to present each word:

- Write the word on the board. Then read the definition and the example sentence, explaining as needed before conducting oral activities.

- Make an overhead transparency of the lesson page that shows the word. Then guide students through the definition, example sentence, and oral activities.

- Reproduce the dictionary on pages 148–159 for each student, or provide each student with a student practice book. (See inside front cover.) Have students find the word in their dictionaries, and then guide them through the definition, example sentence, and oral activities.

A WORD A DAY

End-of-Week Review

Review the four words of the week through oral and written activities designed to reinforce student understanding.

Oral Review
Four oral activities provide you with prompts to review the week's words.

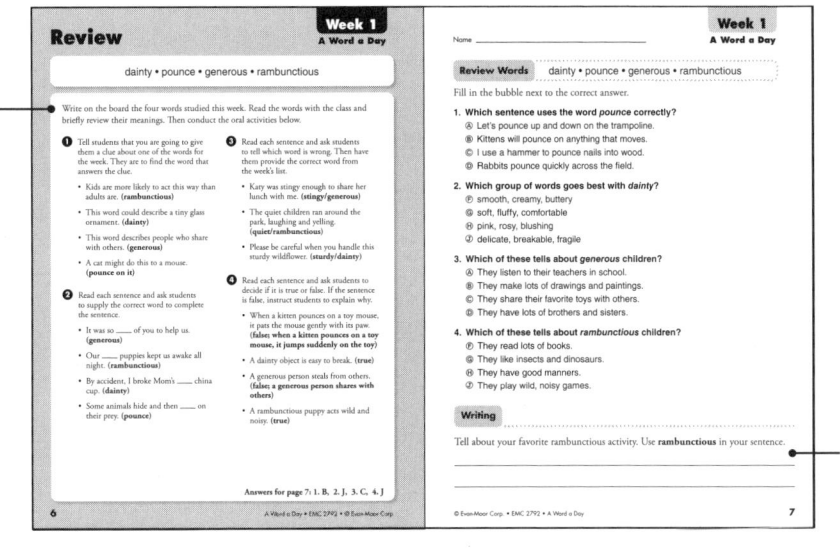

Written Assessment
A student reproducible containing four multiple-choice items and an open-ended writing activity can be used to assess students' mastery.

Additional Features

- Reproducible student dictionary
- Cumulative word index

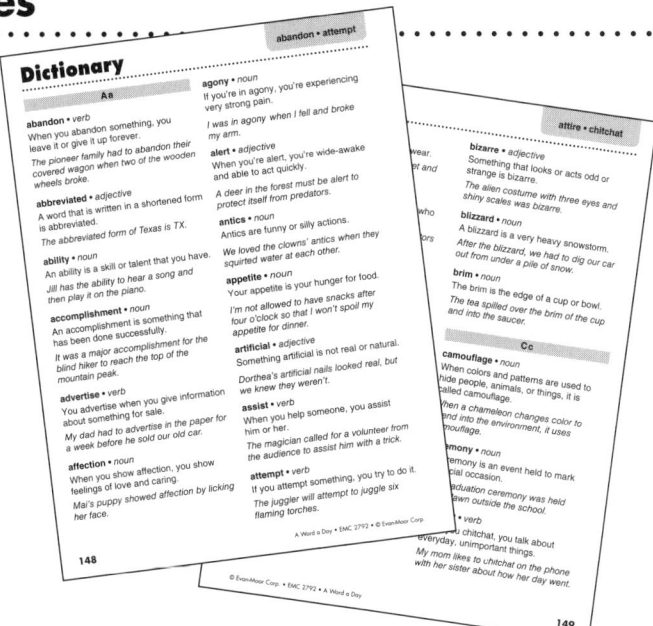

© Evan-Moor Corp. • EMC 2792 • A Word a Day

3

Week 1
A Word a Day

dainty

adjective

Something is **dainty** when it is very delicate.

The **dainty** tea cakes crumbled when I dropped them.

Which of these are **dainty**?
- a wrestler
- a rosebud
- the lace on a baby's dress
- a fine china teacup
- an elephant

Find something **dainty** in the classroom.
What is something **dainty** that you have at home?

pounce

verb

You **pounce** when you jump on something suddenly.

The deer got away before the crouching mountain lion could **pounce** on it.

Which words go with **pounce**?
- leap
- sit
- stand
- jump
- sleep

Do you think it's a good idea to **pounce** on another person? Why or why not?

Week 1
A Word a Day

generous

adjective

A person who is willing to share with others is **generous**.

> The **generous** man shared his prize money with his friends.

Would you be **generous** if you:
- shared your candy bar with a friend?
- spent your allowance on a gift for your sister?
- got a new scooter that you would not let your best friend ride?
- ate a bag of chips by yourself while your hungry friends watched?
- let someone else have the piece of your birthday cake with the rose on it?

Tell about something **generous** that someone did for you. What is something **generous** that you have done for somebody? How did it make you feel?

rambunctious

adjective

When you act wild and noisy, you are being **rambunctious**.

> The children were being so **rambunctious** that the librarian asked them to go outside.

Which ones are acting **rambunctious**?
- Grandma and Grandpa going for a quiet walk
- children playing a game of tag
- puppies fighting over a bone
- the audience at a piano recital
- clowns at a circus performance

Tell about a time when you were acting **rambunctious**. What were you doing? What happened?

Review

Week 1
A Word a Day

dainty • pounce • generous • rambunctious

Write on the board the four words studied this week. Read the words with the class and briefly review their meanings. Then conduct the oral activities below.

1 Tell students that you are going to give them a clue about one of the words for the week. They are to find the word that answers the clue.

- Kids are more likely to act this way than adults are. **(rambunctious)**
- This word could describe a tiny glass ornament. **(dainty)**
- This word describes people who share with others. **(generous)**
- A cat might do this to a mouse. **(pounce on it)**

2 Read each sentence and ask students to supply the correct word to complete the sentence.

- It was so ____ of you to help us. **(generous)**
- Our ____ puppies kept us awake all night. **(rambunctious)**
- By accident, I broke Mom's ____ china cup. **(dainty)**
- Some animals hide and then ____ on their prey. **(pounce)**

3 Read each sentence and ask students to tell which word is wrong. Then have them provide the correct word from the week's list.

- Katy was stingy enough to share her lunch with me. **(stingy/generous)**
- The quiet children ran around the park, laughing and yelling. **(quiet/rambunctious)**
- Please be careful when you handle this sturdy wildflower. **(sturdy/dainty)**

4 Read each sentence and ask students to decide if it is true or false. If the sentence is false, instruct students to explain why.

- When a kitten pounces on a toy mouse, it pats the mouse gently with its paw. **(false; when a kitten pounces on a toy mouse, it jumps suddenly on the toy)**
- A dainty object is easy to break. **(true)**
- A generous person steals from others. **(false; a generous person shares with others)**
- A rambunctious puppy acts wild and noisy. **(true)**

Answers for page 7: 1. B, 2. J, 3. C, 4. J

Name _____

Week 1
A Word a Day

Review Words dainty • pounce • generous • rambunctious

Fill in the bubble next to the correct answer.

1. Which sentence uses the word *pounce* correctly?
- Ⓐ Let's pounce up and down on the trampoline.
- Ⓑ Kittens will pounce on anything that moves.
- Ⓒ I use a hammer to pounce nails into wood.
- Ⓓ Rabbits pounce quickly across the field.

2. Which group of words goes best with *dainty*?
- Ⓕ smooth, creamy, buttery
- Ⓖ soft, fluffy, comfortable
- Ⓗ pink, rosy, blushing
- Ⓙ delicate, breakable, fragile

3. Which of these tells about *generous* children?
- Ⓐ They listen to their teachers in school.
- Ⓑ They make lots of drawings and paintings.
- Ⓒ They share their favorite toys with others.
- Ⓓ They have lots of brothers and sisters.

4. Which of these tells about *rambunctious* children?
- Ⓕ They read lots of books.
- Ⓖ They like insects and dinosaurs.
- Ⓗ They have good manners.
- Ⓙ They play wild, noisy games.

Writing

Tell about your favorite rambunctious activity. Use **rambunctious** in your sentence.

_____

_____

© Evan-Moor Corp. • EMC 2792 • A Word a Day

Week 2
A Word a Day

inquire

verb

When you **inquire**, you try to find out something by asking a question.

For information on when the movie begins, you can **inquire** at the ticket window.

Are you **inquiring** when you:
- call your grandma to wish her a happy birthday?
- ask a librarian where to find a book?
- call your friend to ask when his party starts?
- ask your mom to check your homework?
- ask someone for directions to a new store?

Do you think it's a good idea to **inquire** when you aren't sure about something? Why or why not?

clench

verb

You **clench** something when you squeeze it tightly.

The baseball player **clenched** the bat as he stepped up to home plate.

Which of these could you **clench**?
- a hammer when you're building a bookcase
- a hot dog at a picnic
- your teeth during a scary movie
- a fragile cup as you drink tea
- your friend's arm on a roller coaster ride

When do you **clench** your teeth?
When do you **clench** your fists?

Week 2
A Word a Day

monotone

noun

When you speak in a **monotone**, you don't use any expression in your voice.

> The speaker's **monotone** almost put the audience to sleep.

Which of the following might sound like a **monotone**?

- words spoken by a computer
- a dramatic poem read by its author
- an electronic voice on an answering machine
- a person calling out for help
- someone telling a joke

Say your name, age, favorite color, and favorite food in a **monotone**. Then try it again with lots of expression. Which do you prefer? Why?

attire

noun

Your **attire** is the clothing you wear.

> The proper **attire** for the banquet and dance is a suit or a gown.

Which of these could be part of a bride's **attire**?

- a white gown
- hiking boots
- a baseball cap
- a veil
- high-heeled shoes

What was your **attire** the last time you had to dress up for a special occasion?

Review

Week 2
A Word a Day

inquire • clench • monotone • attire

Write on the board the four words studied this week. Read the words with the class and briefly review their meanings. Then conduct the oral activities below.

1 Tell students that you are going to give them a clue about one of the words for the week. They are to find the word that answers the clue.

- You might do this with your fists if you felt angry. **(clench them)**
- A person just learning to read might use this kind of voice. **(a monotone)**
- You might do this if you wanted information. **(inquire)**
- You must choose this before you go to a party. **(your attire)**

2 Read each sentence and ask students to supply the correct word to complete the sentence.

- The robot speaks in a ____. **(monotone)**
- When practicing your handwriting, don't ____ the pencil. **(clench)**
- When I got lost, I had to ____ about directions. **(inquire)**
- Danny wasn't wearing proper school ____. **(attire)**

3 Read each sentence and ask students to tell which word or words are wrong. Then have them provide the correct word from the week's list.

- Please answer if you want to know where to find something. **(answer/inquire)**
- The dentist asked the patient to relax his teeth. **(relax/clench)**
- When I feel bored, I speak in a voice that is full of expression. **(a voice that is full of expression/a monotone)**

4 Read each sentence and ask students to decide if it is true or false. If the sentence is false, instruct students to explain why.

- Bathing suits and sandals are proper school attire. **(false; this is not proper school clothing)**
- Someone who feels excited probably talks in a monotone. **(false; an excited person would probably speak with lots of expression)**
- A small child who is afraid might clench his father's hand. **(true)**
- The word *inquire* has about the same meaning as *ask*. **(true)**

Answers for page 11: 1. B, 2. J, 3. A, 4. G

Name _____

Week 2
A Word a Day

Review Words   inquire • clench • monotone • attire

Fill in the bubble next to the correct answer.

1. Which sentence uses the word *attire* correctly?
  Ⓐ What is the proper attire for this recipe?
  Ⓑ The queen wore silk, satin, and velvet attire.
  Ⓒ During art class, I painted a colorful attire.
  Ⓓ Our living room sofa has a soft green attire.

2. If you *inquire* about the time, you ___.
  Ⓕ tell someone what time it is
  Ⓖ learn how to tell time
  Ⓗ don't care what time it is
  Ⓙ ask someone what time it is

3. The word *monotone* tells about the way someone ___.
  Ⓐ speaks
  Ⓑ acts
  Ⓒ feels
  Ⓓ moves

4. Which sentence uses the word *clench* correctly?
  Ⓕ Please clench your hair before you go to school.
  Ⓖ I clench my teeth when I feel frightened.
  Ⓗ Did you clench your hands with soap and hot water?
  Ⓙ Clench the cat gently to make it relax in your lap.

Writing

Tell why someone might talk in a monotone. Use **monotone** in your sentence.

_____

_____

Week 3
A Word a Day

spectator

noun

A **spectator** is a person who watches an event without participating in it.

I usually like to play basketball, but today I'm going to be a **spectator** in the stands.

Which of these are **spectators**?

- a father at his daughter's soccer game
- the catcher on a baseball team
- a sports reporter at the Olympics
- a runner in a race
- a tennis player on the court

Which sport do you enjoy as a **spectator**?
Which sport do you enjoy as a player?

omit

verb

When you **omit** something, you leave it out.

If you **omit** your name on your book report, your teacher won't know whose it is.

Which one of these is OK to **omit**?

- the day of the week when you write the date
- a letter in a word on a spelling test
- the time of your birthday party on your invitations
- one of the numbers in your telephone number
- your middle name when you write your name on your paper

When you tell your family about your day at school, what information might you **omit**? What information would you share?

Week 3
A Word a Day

brim

noun

The **brim** is the edge of a cup or bowl.

The tea spilled over the **brim** of the cup and into the saucer.

Which of the following could you fill to the **brim**?

- a soup bowl
- a pencil
- a bucket
- a fork
- a coffee mug

What would you do if your juice glass was filled to the **brim**?

grumble

verb

When you **grumble**, you complain in a grumpy way.

My brother always **grumbles** when Mom reminds him to do his chores.

Which of these would make you **grumble**?

- having to get up early to take out the garbage
- getting ten dollars from Grandpa for your birthday
- being invited to the movies
- having to stay in during recess and clean the desks
- forgetting to take your lunch to school

What is something you **grumble** about?
What is something you have heard someone else **grumble** about?

Review

Week 3
A Word a Day

spectator • omit • brim • grumble

Write on the board the four words studied this week. Read the words with the class and briefly review their meanings. Then conduct the oral activities below.

❶ Tell students that you are going to give them a clue about one of the words for the week. They are to find the word that answers the clue.

- A cup or a glass has one. **(a brim)**
- You might do this if you felt grumpy. **(grumble)**
- If you have ever been to a ballgame, you have been one of these. **(a spectator)**
- When you leave something out, you do this to it. **(omit it)**

❷ Read each sentence and ask students to supply the correct word to complete the sentence.

- A ____ at the game cheered loudly for his team. **(spectator)**
- If you don't like sweet cereal, you can ____ the sugar. **(omit)**
- After it rained, the fishpond was filled to the ____. **(brim)**
- Please don't ____ about having to do your homework. **(grumble)**

❸ Read each sentence and ask students to tell which word or words are wrong. Then have them provide the correct word from the week's list.

- Your story will not make sense if you include the ending. **(include/omit)**
- I filled my glass all the way to the bottom. **(bottom/brim)**
- When he feels grumpy, Pablo talks cheerfully about his chores. **(talks cheerfully/grumbles)**

❹ Read each sentence and ask students to decide if it is true or false. If the sentence is false, instruct students to explain why.

- If you omit a word when you write a sentence, the sentence may not make sense. **(true)**
- A person who grumbles probably feels grumpy about having to do something. **(true)**
- A cup's brim is its handle. **(false; a cup's brim is its edge)**
- The word *spectator* has about the same meaning as *watcher*. **(true)**

Answers for page 15: 1. D, 2. H, 3. A, 4. J

Week 3
A Word a Day

Name _____

Review Words spectator • omit • brim • grumble

Fill in the bubble next to the correct answer.

1. Which sentence uses the word *omit* correctly?
   - Ⓐ Please omit your name at the top of this page.
   - Ⓑ Many people omit dinner at six o'clock in the evening.
   - Ⓒ When I omit a mistake, I try to correct it right away.
   - Ⓓ Please omit the salt. I don't like salty popcorn.

2. When you *grumble* about something, you ___.
   - Ⓕ tell exactly what it is like
   - Ⓖ explain why you like it
   - Ⓗ complain about it grumpily
   - Ⓙ ask a question about it

3. When you fill a cup to the *brim*, you ___.
   - Ⓐ fill it all the way up
   - Ⓑ pour juice out of it
   - Ⓒ fill it only halfway
   - Ⓓ pour in a few drops

4. What does a *spectator* do at a football game?
   - Ⓕ coaches the players
   - Ⓖ plays in the game
   - Ⓗ sells food and drinks
   - Ⓙ watches the game

Writing

Tell what you said the last time you grumbled about something. Use **grumble** in your sentence.

_____

_____

Week 4
A Word a Day

topple

verb

When something **topples**, it falls over.

> The tree was about to **topple** over in the strong wind.

Which things could **topple** easily?
- a large stone statue
- a house
- a child learning to ride a bike
- a tower of building blocks
- a car

How would you stand in order to keep someone from **toppling** you?

zany

adjective

A person who acts **zany** behaves in a foolish or silly way.

> The **zany** clown was honking a giant horn and squirting water from a flower on his coat.

Which words describe someone who acts **zany**?
- calm
- wacky
- nutty
- serious
- angry

Do you like acting **zany** or being around someone who's acting **zany**? Why or why not?

Week 4
A Word a Day

putrid

adjective

If something is **putrid**, it is rotten and smells awful.

After sitting in the sun for two days, the garbage was **putrid**.

Which of these might smell **putrid**?

- the town dump
- a compost pile
- a flower garden
- spoiled milk
- freshly baked bread

Have you ever smelled something **putrid**? What was it? What did you do?

echo

noun

An **echo** is a sound that repeats because it bounces off a large surface.

After I yelled down to the hikers at the bottom of the canyon, the **echo** of my voice came back: "Hello . . . hello . . . hello . . ."

In which of these places might you hear an **echo**?

- the halls of an empty building
- a mountain overlooking a valley
- a crowded department store
- your bedroom
- a long tunnel

If you were in a place that made a good **echo**, what would you like to say?

Review

Week 4
A Word a Day

topple • zany • putrid • echo

Write on the board the four words studied this week. Read the words with the class and briefly review their meanings. Then conduct the oral activities below.

❶ Tell students that you are going to give them a clue about one of the words for the week. They are to find the word that answers the clue.

- You might laugh when someone acts this way. (**zany**)
- A tower of empty soda cans might do this. (**topple**)
- If you left a glass of milk in the sun for a week, it would smell this way. (**putrid**)
- This might be the result of yelling inside a cave. (**an echo**)

❷ Read each sentence and ask students to supply the correct word to complete the sentence.

- A driver honked his horn in the tunnel to make an ___. (**echo**)
- It is not usually OK to act ___ inside the classroom. (**zany**)
- Mr. Pine bumped into a stack of shoeboxes and caused it to ___ over. (**topple**)
- When I opened the garbage can, it smelled ___ inside. (**putrid**)

❸ Read each sentence and ask students to tell which word or words are wrong. Then have them provide the correct word from the week's list.

- I hate the fragrant smell of rotten vegetables. (**fragrant/putrid**)
- Mateo's serious behavior makes everyone giggle. (**serious/zany**)
- My baby sister piles up blocks and then whacks the pile to make it rise up. (**rise up/topple over**)

❹ Read each sentence and ask students to decide if it is true or false. If the sentence is false, instruct students to explain why.

- An echo is a kind of bird. (**false; an echo is a sound that repeats**)
- A strong wind can make a tree topple over. (**true**)
- The word *putrid* has about the same meaning as *fresh*. (**false; *putrid* means about the same as *rotten***)
- The word *zany* has about the same meaning as *silly*. (**true**)

Answers for page 19: 1. C, 2. F, 3. B, 4. F

Name _____

Week 4
A Word a Day

Review Words   topple • zany • putrid • echo

Fill in the bubble next to the correct answer.

1. Which sentence uses the word *topple* correctly?
- Ⓐ If you set an ice cube in the sun, it will topple.
- Ⓑ It is polite to topple your friend when he speaks.
- Ⓒ The boxes will topple if you put the small ones on the bottom.
- Ⓓ Please topple over to my house sometime soon.

2. If you saw someone acting *zany*, you would probably ___.
- Ⓕ laugh
- Ⓖ cry
- Ⓗ yell for help
- Ⓙ try to comfort the person

3. An *echo* is a sound that bounces back and ___.
- Ⓐ is silent
- Ⓑ repeats
- Ⓒ goes up and down
- Ⓓ gets louder and louder

4. Which of these smells *putrid*?
- Ⓕ rotten meat
- Ⓖ fresh fruit
- Ⓗ toothpaste
- Ⓙ clean clothes

Writing

Write about a time when you heard an echo. Use **echo** in your sentence.

_____

_____

© Evan-Moor Corp. • EMC 2792 • A Word a Day

Week 5
A Word a Day

infant

noun

An **infant** is a baby.

The **infant** was sleeping peacefully in her crib.

Which words can describe an **infant**?

- tiny
- mighty
- mean
- precious
- noisy

Do you have any pictures of yourself as an **infant**? Tell about one of them.

ability

noun

An **ability** is a skill or talent that you have.

Jill has the **ability** to hear a song and then play it on the piano.

Which of these take a special **ability**?

- breathing
- singing
- playing a violin
- eating
- winning a chess tournament

What special **ability** do you have? Which would you like to have?

Tell about someone you know who has a special **ability**.

Week 5
A Word a Day

dynamo

noun

A **dynamo** is an active person with lots of energy and enthusiasm.

Diana is a **dynamo**, performing in the school show, playing on a soccer team, and belonging to two clubs!

Would you be a **dynamo** if you:
- slept until noon all summer?
- ran around the track more times than the coach asked you to?
- organized a recycling project at your school?
- moved as slowly as a snail?
- led the cheering section for the football team?

Are you a **dynamo**, or do you know someone who is? What makes you or the person you know a **dynamo**?

trivial

adjective

When something is **trivial**, it has little importance.

Your book report doesn't need to mention the number of illustrations in the story. That's **trivial** information.

Which of the following information about you is **trivial**?
- your name
- the number of times you blinked your eyes today
- your birthday
- the color of your socks
- your phone number

Share some **trivial** information about yourself or your family with the class.

Review

Week 5
A Word a Day

infant • ability • dynamo • trivial

Write on the board the four words studied this week. Read the words with the class and briefly review their meanings. Then conduct the oral activities below.

❶ Tell students that you are going to give them a clue about one of the words for the week. They are to find the word that answers the clue.

- You were one of these when you were born. **(an infant)**
- This word names someone who is full of energy. **(a dynamo)**
- This is the skill or talent to do something. **(ability)**
- This word tells about a fact that isn't very important. **(trivial)**

❷ Read each sentence and ask students to supply the correct word to complete the sentence.

- Please don't bother me with ___ information when I'm busy. **(trivial)**
- Leo is a ___ who is involved in many activities. **(dynamo)**
- My cousin's baby is the cutest ___ I've ever seen. **(infant)**
- Dad is known in the neighborhood for his ___ to bake yummy cookies. **(ability)**

❸ Read each sentence and ask students to tell which word or words are wrong. Then have them provide the correct word from the week's list.

- Important details do not matter very much. **(Important/Trivial)**
- An adult cannot yet walk. **(adult/infant)**
- Ms. Raymer is a lazy person who works hard all day. **(lazy person/dynamo)**
- Matty has the clumsiness to juggle five oranges at once. **(clumsiness/ability)**

❹ Read each sentence and ask students to decide if it is true or false. If the sentence is false, instruct students to explain why.

- A dynamo rests or sleeps most of the time. **(false; a dynamo is an energetic person)**
- A person with drawing skill has the ability to draw well. **(true)**
- The word *infant* means *baby*. **(true)**
- Your age is a trivial piece of information about you. **(false; your age is an important piece of information about you)**

Answers for page 23: 1. B, 2. F, 3. C, 4. J

Name _____

Week 5
A Word a Day

Review Words   infant • ability • dynamo • trivial

Fill in the bubble next to the correct answer.

1. **Which sentence uses the word *ability* correctly?**
   - Ⓐ It was my ability to name our new puppy "Minka."
   - Ⓑ Do dogs have the ability to understand human speech?
   - Ⓒ In my ability, you shouldn't feed table scraps to dogs.
   - Ⓓ My dog Daisy and I have great ability for each other.

2. **That *infant* is about ___ old.**
   - Ⓕ five months
   - Ⓖ five years
   - Ⓗ ten years
   - Ⓙ fifteen years

3. **A *dynamo* is someone who has lots of ___.**
   - Ⓐ clothes
   - Ⓑ money
   - Ⓒ energy
   - Ⓓ friends

4. **Which sentence tells about *trivial* information?**
   - Ⓕ It is about the past.
   - Ⓖ It is about the future.
   - Ⓗ It is very, very important.
   - Ⓙ It is not very important.

Writing

Tell about an infant you know. Use **infant** in your sentence.

_____

_____

© Evan-Moor Corp. • EMC 2792 • A Word a Day

23

Week 6
A Word a Day

camouflage

noun

When colors and patterns are used to hide people, animals, or things, it is called **camouflage**.

When a chameleon changes color to blend into the environment, it uses **camouflage**.

Which animals use **camouflage**?
- a polar bear in white snow
- a spotted cow in a green pasture
- a green lizard on a green leaf
- a red rooster on a white fence
- a spotted leopard in shaded grass

If you wanted to use **camouflage** in the woods, what would you wear? Do you think wearing **camouflage** is a good idea? Why?

hue

noun

A **hue** is a color or a shade of a color.

I couldn't decide whether to color the flower a light or dark red **hue**.

"Strawberry red" and "rose red" are the names of **hues**. Choose a descriptive name for each of these **hues**:
- light blue
- dark yellow
- bright orange
- light pink
- medium green

A rainbow has seven colors. What are they? Which **hue** is your favorite? What do you own in that **hue**?

Week 6
A Word a Day

wince

verb

You **wince** when you pull back or make a face in fear, pain, or dislike.

I **wince** every time my pet snake eats a mouse.

Would you **wince** if you:

- got an A on a test?
- were getting a shot?
- were having a birthday party?
- had to take bad-tasting medicine?
- had your tooth drilled by the dentist?

Describe a situation that makes you **wince**.

compromise

verb

When both sides give in a little to settle a disagreement, they **compromise**.

When Linda wanted to read and Janie wanted to watch a video, they **compromised** by listening to an audiobook.

In which of these situations could people **compromise**?

- You're invited to a beach party on the day of your family reunion.
- Your brother wants macaroni, but you want pizza.
- Your dad gets a $25 traffic ticket, but he only wants to pay $10.
- Half the class wants to play tag, but the others want to play ball.
- Mom wants to go to Hawaii, but Dad wants to go hiking.

Choose one of the situations listed above and tell how the people might **compromise**.

Review

Week 6
A Word a Day

camouflage • hue • wince • compromise

Write on the board the four words studied this week. Read the words with the class and briefly review their meanings. Then conduct the oral activities below.

❶ Tell students that you are going to give them a clue about one of the words for the week. They are to find the word that answers the clue.

- Since a polar bear lives in a snowy place, the bear's white fur gives it this. **(camouflage)**
- You might do this if you see something creepy. **(wince)**
- Bright pink is one. **(a hue)**
- You do this when you and another person each give something up to settle an argument. **(compromise)**

❷ Read each sentence and ask students to supply the correct word to complete the sentence.

- If we ____, we will each get part of what we want. **(compromise)**
- I painted the grass a bright yellow-green ____. **(hue)**
- I ____ when I see other people hurt themselves. **(wince)**
- A lion's fur color matches its habitat and gives it ____. **(camouflage)**

❸ Read each sentence and ask students to tell which word or words are wrong. Then have them provide the correct word from the week's list.

- I smile with fear when I hear a loud crack of lightning. **(smile/wince)**
- People refuse to give in when they settle an argument. **(refuse to give in/compromise)**
- The Arctic fox's white fur gives it a way to stand out in the winter snow. **(a way to stand out/camouflage)**

❹ Read each sentence and ask students to decide if it is true or false. If the sentence is false, instruct students to explain why.

- Someone who winces is probably afraid or in pain. **(true)**
- A soldier's uniform may have colorful blotches for camouflage. **(true)**
- Midnight blue is a hue. **(true)**
- When two people compromise, they refuse to give up anything. **(false; they each give up part of what they want in order to settle an argument)**

Answers for page 27: 1. C, 2. J, 3. B, 4. G

Week 6
A Word a Day

Name _____

Review Words camouflage • hue • wince • compromise

Fill in the bubble next to the correct answer.

1. **Which sentence uses the word *wince* correctly?**
   - Ⓐ I wince when someone tells a funny joke.
   - Ⓑ When we hear good news, we wince with joy.
   - Ⓒ I wince whenever the doctor gives me a shot.
   - Ⓓ Our dogs wince their tails to say hello to us.

2. ***Camouflage* helps an animal to ___.**
   - Ⓕ keep warm
   - Ⓖ sleep
   - Ⓗ find water
   - Ⓙ hide

3. **Which of these is a *hue*?**
   - Ⓐ the sky
   - Ⓑ sky blue
   - Ⓒ grass
   - Ⓓ a lawn

4. **Which group of words tells about *compromising*?**
   - Ⓕ celebration, festival, banquet
   - Ⓖ agreement, settlement, cooperation
   - Ⓗ warning, emergency, danger
   - Ⓙ disagreement, argument, quarrel

Writing

Tell about a time when you and another person compromised. Use **compromise** in your sentence.

_____

_____

Week 7
A Word a Day

flimsy

adjective

Something that is weak and lightweight is **flimsy**.

> The weight of the books caused the **flimsy** box to break when I picked it up.

Which of these are **flimsy**?

- a brick
- the bathroom sink
- a piece of tracing paper
- a spider web
- a bronze statue

Find something in the class that is **flimsy**. Find something else that is not. Compare the two things. How are they alike and how are they different?

grant

verb

When you **grant** something to a person, you allow him or her to have it.

> The fairy waved her magic wand and said, "I will **grant** you one wish."

Which of these could someone really **grant**?

- permission to leave class to get a drink of water
- a license to fly a space shuttle
- permission to live 200 years
- a license to fish in a stream or an ocean
- permission to stay up late on the weekend

Imagine that you have been magically transported into a fairy tale. A genie pops out of a lamp and will **grant** you three wishes. What will you wish for and why?

Week 7
A Word a Day

talented

adjective

When you have a natural ability to do something well, you are **talented**.

> The **talented** young singer sang as well as a professional recording artist.

Would you need to be **talented** in order to:

- tie your shoelaces?
- play in an orchestra?
- paint a picture that was shown in a museum?
- sharpen a pencil?
- juggle three flaming torches?

If you could be **talented** at anything in the world, what would it be? Explain your answer. What are you already **talented** at?

opinion

noun

Your **opinion** is what you think about something.

> I thought the movie would be exciting, but I changed my **opinion** after I saw it.

Which of these are **opinions**?

- The sun rises in the morning.
- Your teacher is smart.
- People have to eat to stay alive.
- Red is the best color.
- Spelling is fun.

Share your **opinion** about these ideas:

- Students should be given more homework.
- Students should have longer recesses.
- It's fun to do chores.

Review

Week 7
A Word a Day

flimsy • grant • talented • opinion

Write on the board the four words studied this week. Read the words with the class and briefly review their meanings. Then conduct the oral activities below.

1 Tell students that you are going to give them a clue about one of the words for the week. They are to find the word that answers the clue.

- This word describes someone who is a good artist or good at sports. **(talented)**
- This word describes the first little pig's straw house. **(flimsy)**
- When you say what you think about something, you tell this. **(an opinion)**
- This word has about the same meaning as *give*. **(grant)**

2 Read each sentence and ask students to supply the correct word to complete the sentence.

- In Robyn's ___, mustard yellow is an ugly color. **(opinion)**
- Don't use ___ materials to build your treehouse. **(flimsy)**
- Adam is a ___ singer who also plays the guitar. **(talented)**
- I hope Mom will ___ me permission to go on the camping trip. **(grant)**

3 Read each sentence and ask students to tell which word or words are wrong. Then have them provide the correct word from the week's list.

- If you call something "good" or "bad," you are giving a fact. **(a fact/an opinion)**
- Mary is an unskilled ballerina who dances beautifully. **(an unskilled/a talented)**
- The second pig used thin, weak sticks to build a strong, sturdy house. **(strong, sturdy/flimsy)**
- Of course you may go! I deny my permission. **(deny/grant)**

4 Read each sentence and ask students to decide if it is true or false. If the sentence is false, instruct students to explain why.

- It is easy to tear flimsy cloth. **(true)**
- Opinions might include words like *boring* and *interesting*. **(true)**
- A talented cook can make delicious meals. **(true)**
- If someone grants you a favor, he or she refuses to do it. **(false; someone who grants you a favor agrees to do it)**

Answers for page 31: 1. C, 2. H, 3. D, 4. F

30

A Word a Day • EMC 2792 • © Evan-Moor Corp.

Name _____

Week 7
A Word a Day

Review Words flimsy • grant • talented • opinion

Fill in the bubble next to the correct answer.

1. Which sentence uses the word *talented* correctly?
- Ⓐ Now that it is painted, our home looks talented.
- Ⓑ I'm talented because I exercise and eat right.
- Ⓒ Amy is a talented artist who paints beautiful pictures.
- Ⓓ Alex made this talented drawing of an airplane.

2. When you give your *opinion* of a movie, you tell ___.
- Ⓕ the title and the actors in the movie
- Ⓖ untrue information about the movie
- Ⓗ what you thought about the movie
- Ⓙ where you saw the movie

3. When your teacher *grants* you permission to do something, she ___.
- Ⓐ asks you what you want to do
- Ⓑ does not let you do it
- Ⓒ wonders if it is a good idea
- Ⓓ allows you to do it

4. Which group of words goes best with *flimsy*?
- Ⓕ weak, lightweight, easy to break
- Ⓖ floppy, shaggy, not brushed
- Ⓗ dangerous, unsafe, harmful
- Ⓙ grumpy, grouchy, unfriendly

Writing

Give your opinion of the last movie you saw or the last story you read. Use **opinion** in your sentence.

_____

_____

© Evan-Moor Corp. • EMC 2792 • A Word a Day

Week 8
A Word a Day

obnoxious

adjective

When something is disagreeable and unpleasant, it is **obnoxious**.

The play was ruined by some **obnoxious** people in the audience who were talking during the show.

Which of the following are examples of **obnoxious** behavior?

- throwing food at your friends during lunch
- sitting quietly and reading a book
- bringing a nice gift to a birthday party
- grabbing a book out of someone's hands
- singing loudly in the library

Have you ever seen someone being **obnoxious**? What was the person doing? How did you feel about it?

scholar

noun

A **scholar** is a person who has studied and learned a lot.

Professor Rossi, a famous music **scholar**, knows about all kinds of music.

Which of these would a **scholar** probably do?

- get to class late
- spend time in the library
- play in a rock-and-roll band
- enjoy reading and writing
- discuss interesting ideas

How are you like a **scholar**? In what ways could you be a better **scholar**?

Week 8
A Word a Day

vigorous

adjective

When something is **vigorous**, it is strong, active, and full of energy.

Vigorous exercise makes your heart work harder.

Which of the following are **vigorous**?
- a weight lifter
- a patient in the hospital
- a firefighter
- a sleeping baby
- a playful puppy

What is your favorite **vigorous** activity? What do you enjoy about it?

etiquette

noun

The rules of polite behavior, especially for social situations, are called **etiquette**.

It is good **etiquette** to chew with your mouth closed.

Which statements show good **etiquette**?
- Sit up straight at the dinner table.
- Throw any food you don't like on the floor.
- Talk with your mouth full of food.
- Keep your napkin on your lap when you're not using it.
- Remember to say "please" and "thank you."

What are some rules of **etiquette** that you follow?

Review

Week 8
A Word a Day

obnoxious • scholar • vigorous • etiquette

Write on the board the four words studied this week. Read the words with the class and briefly review their meanings. Then conduct the oral activities below.

1 Tell students that you are going to give them a clue about one of the words for the week. They are to find the word that answers the clue.

- This kind of behavior bothers other people. **(obnoxious)**
- Swimming and tennis are examples of this kind of exercise. **(vigorous)**
- This person might be an expert on a certain topic. **(a scholar)**
- You might need to learn more about this before going to a fancy party. **(etiquette)**

2 Read each sentence and ask students to supply the correct word to complete the sentence.

- Ms. Asher is an art ____ who studies French paintings. **(scholar)**
- It is good ____ to thank people who give you gifts. **(etiquette)**
- Swimming can be ____ exercise. **(vigorous)**
- Scribbling in a library book is ____ behavior. **(obnoxious)**

3 Read each sentence and ask students to tell which word or words are wrong. Then have them provide the correct word from the week's list.

- This book on bad behavior tells how to act politely. **(bad behavior/etiquette)**
- We don't like being around people with pleasant behavior! **(pleasant/obnoxious)**
- Running, biking, and soccer are restful activities. **(restful/vigorous)**

4 Read each sentence and ask students to decide if it is true or false. If the sentence is false, instruct students to explain why.

- Vigorous exercise might make someone sweat. **(true)**
- A scholar is mainly interested in games. **(false; a scholar is mainly interested in studying)**
- Obnoxious behavior can make others mad at you. **(true)**
- A book on etiquette might tell you how to act at a wedding. **(true)**

Answers for page 35: 1. C, 2. H, 3. A, 4. G

Week 8
A Word a Day

Name _____

Review Words: obnoxious • scholar • vigorous • etiquette

Fill in the bubble next to the correct answer.

1. Which sentence tells about *obnoxious* behavior?
   - Ⓐ My grandma gave me a birthday present.
   - Ⓑ My brother was sick, so he stayed home from school.
   - Ⓒ Our neighbors played loud music until late at night.
   - Ⓓ Dad made chicken and vegetables for dinner last night.

2. It is good *etiquette* to ___.
   - Ⓕ get up very early on weekends
   - Ⓖ interrupt someone who is saying something boring
   - Ⓗ say "excuse me" when you bump into someone
   - Ⓙ read books that give interesting information

3. Which tells about *vigorous* activity?
   - Ⓐ playing basketball
   - Ⓑ reading a book
   - Ⓒ getting into bed
   - Ⓓ petting your dog

4. Which person is a *scholar*?
   - Ⓕ a girl who plays on the best soccer team in town
   - Ⓖ a college teacher who studies and teaches history
   - Ⓗ a boy who wants to be a firefighter someday
   - Ⓙ a woman who owns three grocery stores in town

Writing

Tell about a time when you did (or did not) practice good etiquette. Use **etiquette** in your sentence.

_____

_____

Week 9
A Word a Day

disturb

verb

You **disturb** people when you bother, annoy, or interrupt them.

> I wanted to read, so I hung a sign on my door that said "Do Not **Disturb**."

Which of these might **disturb** you if you were trying to sleep?

- loud music
- an ambulance siren outside your window
- a leaf falling
- someone snoring loudly across the room
- your dog sleeping in the kitchen

Tell about a time when someone **disturbed** you. What did the person do? How did you feel?

miniature

adjective

Something **miniature** is smaller than its usual size.

> The **miniature** cars in my collection look just like real ones.

Which words describe something that is **miniature**?

- small
- huge
- enormous
- teensy
- little

Do you own anything that is a **miniature** size of a real thing?

Week 9
A Word a Day

bizarre

adjective

Something that looks or acts odd or strange is **bizarre**.

The alien costume with three eyes and shiny scales was **bizarre**.

Would it be **bizarre** if:
- you woke up and were ten feet tall?
- a rabbit liked to eat carrots?
- your pet rat started talking to you?
- the characters in your favorite cartoon came out of the TV?
- the food in your refrigerator was cold?

What is the most **bizarre** thing you've ever seen or heard about?

companion

noun

A **companion** keeps someone company.

The guide dog was the blind woman's constant **companion**.

Which of the following are **companions**?
- a baby sitter and a small child
- a cashier and a customer at a store
- two friends walking together on a beach
- a waiter and a diner at a restaurant
- a pet and its owner

What do you enjoy doing with a **companion**?

Review

Week 9
A Word a Day

disturb • miniature • bizarre • companion

Write on the board the four words studied this week. Read the words with the class and briefly review their meanings. Then conduct the oral activities below.

1 Tell students that you are going to give them a clue about one of the words for the week. They are to find the word that answers the clue.

- If something strange or odd happened, you might use this word to tell about it. **(bizarre)**
- You might use this word to describe a tiny statue of a horse. **(miniature)**
- Being noisy might do this to someone who is studying. **(disturb the person)**
- This is someone who keeps you company. **(a companion)**

2 Read each sentence and ask students to supply the correct word to complete the sentence.

- Please do not ____ me while I'm resting. **(disturb)**
- My dog makes a great ____ on long walks. **(companion)**
- This doll has a ____ umbrella, raincoat, and boots. **(miniature)**
- The actor wore brightly colored clothing that didn't match. He looked ____. **(bizarre)**

3 Read each sentence and ask students to tell which word or words are wrong. Then have them provide the correct word from the week's list.

- This huge toy train came in a small box. **(huge/miniature)**
- Mom asked us not to calm down the baby while she was napping. **(calm down/disturb)**
- It is normal to eat breakfast while standing on your head. **(normal/bizarre)**

4 Read each sentence and ask students to decide if it is true or false. If the sentence is false, instruct students to explain why.

- Bizarre sights may surprise or scare people. **(true)**
- A companion makes you feel lonely. **(false; a companion keeps you company)**
- Disturbing people is a good way to make friends with them. **(false; people don't like being bothered or annoyed)**
- A miniature poodle is smaller than a regular-sized poodle. **(true)**

Answers for page 39: 1. D, 2. H, 3. A, 4. G

Name _____

Week 9
A Word a Day

Review Words | disturb • miniature • bizarre • companion

Fill in the bubble next to the correct answer.

1. Which sentence tells about *bizarre* behavior?
    - Ⓐ My grandma takes me to baseball games.
    - Ⓑ My sister eats peanut butter and jelly sandwiches.
    - Ⓒ My mom works for a telephone company.
    - Ⓓ My brother sleeps on the floor with no blankets.

2. When you *disturb* someone, you ___ that person.
    - Ⓕ help
    - Ⓖ like
    - Ⓗ bother
    - Ⓙ meet

3. Which sentence tells about *miniature* furniture?
    - Ⓐ It fits inside a dollhouse.
    - Ⓑ It is big enough for a giant.
    - Ⓒ It is living room furniture.
    - Ⓓ It is classroom furniture.

4. Which person is your *companion*?
    - Ⓕ your doctor
    - Ⓖ a good friend of yours
    - Ⓗ someone you met once
    - Ⓙ your music teacher

Writing

Tell what it might be like to be miniature—about as tall as a pencil.
Use **miniature** in your sentence.

_____

_____

Week 10
A Word a Day

trio

noun

A **trio** is a group of three.

The three girls called their singing **trio** "Wee Three."

Which of these circus acts would be introduced as a **trio**?

- two men and a woman juggling plates
- a unicycle rider
- three ladies riding horses bareback
- two clowns being shot out of a cannon
- three dancing bears

What activities have you done with two other friends as a **trio**? What activities would be hard to do as a **trio**?

retrieve

verb

When you get something back, you **retrieve** it.

I had to **retrieve** my homework from the trash after I threw it away by mistake.

Which of these could you **retrieve**?

- the food you ate for lunch yesterday
- a book that fell down the stairs
- a newspaper in your recycling bin
- a button that washed down the drain
- the sunset that you watched last week

What is something that you had to **retrieve**? Where did you **retrieve** it from?

Week 10
A Word a Day

alert

adjective

When you're **alert**, you're wide-awake and able to act quickly.

A deer in the forest must be **alert** to protect itself from predators.

Would you be **alert** if:

- you fell asleep in class?
- you caught someone who was trying to sneak up behind you?
- you were the first one to follow the directions and solve a puzzle?
- your mom had to ask you the same question three times?
- you saw smoke coming out of a neighbor's window and called 911?

When is it a good idea to be **alert**?
When is it not so important to be **alert**?

hodgepodge

noun

A **hodgepodge** is a disorderly, jumbled mess of things.

Jimmy could not find his truck in the **hodgepodge** of toys on the floor.

Which of these is a **hodgepodge**?

- a neat stack of books
- a pile of mismatched shoes
- windblown papers all over the floor
- pillows placed neatly on a bed
- scraps of fabric in a ragbag

Which things are in a **hodgepodge** in your room?
Which things are kept neat and tidy?

Review

Week 10
A Word a Day

trio • retrieve • alert • hodgepodge

Write on the board the four words studied this week. Read the words with the class and briefly review their meanings. Then conduct the oral activities below.

1 Tell students that you are going to give them a clue about one of the words for the week. They are to find the word that answers the clue.

- If you accidentally threw something away, you might need to do this. **(retrieve it)**
- This word names a messy bunch of things. **(hodgepodge)**
- Mice have to be this way to protect themselves from cats. **(alert)**
- You and two others could form one of these. **(a trio)**

2 Read each sentence and ask students to supply the correct word to complete the sentence.

- Please ___ the magazine from the recycle bin. **(retrieve)**
- Peter, Paul, and Mary formed a famous singing ___. **(trio)**
- How can you find your sweater in that ___ of clothes? **(hodgepodge)**
- A good watchdog stays ___ and barks when strangers come to the door. **(alert)**

3 Read each sentence and ask students to tell which word or words are wrong. Then have them provide the correct word from the week's list.

- I threw the ball so my dog could take it away. **(take it away/retrieve it)**
- Getting plenty of sleep every night will help you stay sleepy in school. **(sleepy/alert)**
- I can never find a pair of shoes. They are in a neat row on my closet floor. **(neat row/hodgepodge)**

4 Read each sentence and ask students to decide if it is true or false. If the sentence is false, instruct students to explain why.

- A dance trio has three dancers in it. **(true)**
- A hodgepodge is a neatly arranged group of things. **(false; a hodgepodge is a messy collection of things)**
- If you stay alert, you'll be able to act quickly. **(true)**
- When you retrieve something from the recycling bin, you throw it into the bin. **(false; you take it back out of the bin)**

Answers for page 43: 1. B, 2. F, 3. B, 4. G

Week 10
A Word a Day

Name _____

Review Words trio • retrieve • alert • hodgepodge

Fill in the bubble next to the correct answer.

1. **Which sentence tells about a *trio*?**
   - Ⓐ My four friends and I have a secret club.
   - Ⓑ My three cousins sing together in a group.
   - Ⓒ My mom and dad play on a softball team.
   - Ⓓ My brother's band has five musicians in it.

2. **Which words tell about a *hodgepodge*?**
   - Ⓕ a messy pile of mismatched socks
   - Ⓖ a stack of neatly folded clothes
   - Ⓗ two pairs of new school shoes
   - Ⓙ coats and hats hanging in a row

3. **Which sentence uses *alert* correctly?**
   - Ⓐ By ten o'clock at night, I was tired and alert.
   - Ⓑ You can catch every ball if you stay alert.
   - Ⓒ After school, I felt so alert that I needed a snack.
   - Ⓓ Stay alert so that you can fall asleep quickly.

4. **When my dogs *retrieve* toys, they ____.**
   - Ⓕ chew on them and ruin them
   - Ⓖ bring them back to me after I throw them
   - Ⓗ choose the toys that they like best
   - Ⓙ ignore the toys that do not interest them

Writing

Which do you like better, playing with friends in pairs or in trios? Tell why. Use **trio** in your sentence.

_____

_____

Week 11
A Word a Day

affection

noun

When you show **affection**, you show feelings of love and caring.

> Mai's puppy showed **affection** by licking her face.

Which ones show **affection**?

- getting a hug from your mom
- giving someone a valentine
- stepping on someone's toe
- bringing flowers to your grandmother
- borrowing your brother's favorite shirt without asking

What are things that you do to show **affection**?
What are ways **affection** is shown to you?

scarce

adjective

Something is **scarce** if it's hard to get or find.

> Parking spaces were **scarce** at the mall on the day of the big sale.

Which of these might be **scarce**?

- rivers in the desert
- snow on a mountain in winter
- sand on a beach
- gold coins at the bottom of the ocean
- ants at a picnic

What are some things that are **scarce** where we live?

Week 11
A Word a Day

inhabit

verb

You **inhabit** the place where you live.

Bats **inhabit** the caves on this cliff.

Which of these places can people **inhabit**?

- an apartment
- the moon
- a trailer
- a lake
- an island

What are some of the places your family has **inhabited** since you were born?

identical

adjective

When things are exactly alike, they're **identical**.

The twins were **identical**. You could not tell one from the other.

Which words describe things that are **identical**?

- different
- same
- matching
- unusual
- opposite

Do you own anything that's **identical** to something that someone else owns? What is it?

45

Review

Week 11
A Word a Day

affection • scarce • inhabit • identical

Write on the board the four words studied this week. Read the words with the class and briefly review their meanings. Then conduct the oral activities below.

1 Tell students that you are going to give them a clue about one of the words for the week. They are to find the word that answers the clue.

- This word describes things that are exactly the same. **(identical)**
- This word has about the same meaning as *live in*. **(inhabit)**
- This word has about the same meaning as *love*. **(affection)**
- This word could be used to describe the absence of flowers during a snowy winter. **(scarce)**

2 Read each sentence and ask students to supply the correct word to complete the sentence.

- I feel great ____ for my family and friends. **(affection)**
- Hanna and Diana are ____ twins. It is hard to tell which girl is which. **(identical)**
- Squirrels and raccoons ____ my backyard. **(inhabit)**
- When water is ____, we should not water our grass very often. **(scarce)**

3 Read each sentence and ask students to tell which word or words are wrong. Then have them provide the correct word from the week's list.

- In hot, dry deserts, water is plentiful. **(plentiful/scarce)**
- I gave my aunt a hug and a kiss to show my dislike. **(dislike/affection)**
- These shiny new pennies look completely different. **(completely different/identical)**

4 Read each sentence and ask students to decide if it is true or false. If the sentence is false, instruct students to explain why.

- Wild polar bears inhabit tropical rainforests. **(false; wild polar bears live in cold, snowy places)**
- When food is scarce, people can eat as much as they want. **(false; when food is scarce, people don't have much to eat)**
- If there are differences between two things, the two are *not* identical. **(true)**
- Most people feel affection for their pets. **(true)**

Answers for page 47: 1. C, 2. F, 3. C, 4. J

Name _____

Week 11
A Word a Day

Review Words affection • scarce • inhabit • identical

Fill in the bubble next to the correct answer.

1. Which sentence tells about three *identical* pencils?
- Ⓐ One is yellow, one is blue, and one is red.
- Ⓑ Each one is a different length.
- Ⓒ Each one is exactly the same as the others.
- Ⓓ Two are old, and one is brand-new.

2. Which sentence uses *inhabit* correctly?
- Ⓕ Worms inhabit the dirt in my garden.
- Ⓖ After elementary school, children inhabit middle school.
- Ⓗ I like to inhabit the toy store on my way home.
- Ⓙ Birds inhabit the worms in my garden.

3. Which sentence uses *affection* correctly?
- Ⓐ People who show affection are not afraid.
- Ⓑ Ana shows affection by doing her homework.
- Ⓒ My little sister shows affection by hugging us.
- Ⓓ People show affection by yawning loudly.

4. When food is *scarce*, we have ____.
- Ⓕ plenty for everyone to eat
- Ⓖ no food at all
- Ⓗ many different kinds of food
- Ⓙ only a small amount of food

Writing

Do you think identical twins should dress in identical outfits? Tell why or why not. Use **identical** in your sentence.

_____

_____

© Evan-Moor Corp. • EMC 2792 • A Word a Day

Week 12
A Word a Day

participate

verb

When you take part in something, you **participate**.

She didn't want to **participate** in the game, so she just watched.

In which of these can you **participate**?
- a game of dodgeball
- the Olympic games
- a children's sports team
- a motorcycle race
- a spelling bee

What activities do you **participate** in during recess?

decay

verb

When something **decays**, it becomes rotten.

If you don't want your teeth to **decay**, you need to brush them regularly.

Which of these could **decay**?
- a leaf
- a glass of water
- a piece of wood
- a slice of bread
- a windowpane

What can cause your teeth to **decay**?
What do you do so that your teeth won't **decay**?

Week 12
A Word a Day

modern

adjective

Something that is from recent times is **modern**.

Modern refrigerators use much less energy than older ones.

Which of the following are **modern**?

- a covered wagon
- a space shuttle
- a solar-powered car
- a wood-burning stove
- a scooter

What **modern** inventions are a part of your life that did not exist in the days of the Pilgrims? How would your life be different without some of the **modern** inventions we have now?

grip

verb

When you hold something very tightly, you **grip** it.

The climber **gripped** the rope as she made her way up the steep mountain.

Which words mean about the same thing as **grip**?

- hold on
- clutch
- drop
- grab
- let go

Tell about a time when you would have fallen if you hadn't had something to **grip**. Where were you? What did you **grip**?

Review

Week 12
A Word a Day

participate • decay • modern • grip

Write on the board the four words studied this week. Read the words with the class and briefly review their meanings. Then conduct the oral activities below.

❶ Tell students that you are going to give them a clue about one of the words for the week. They are to find the word that answers the clue.

- When you take part in an activity, you do this. **(participate in it)**
- This word means the opposite of *old-fashioned*. **(modern)**
- This word has about the same meaning as *rot*. **(decay)**
- When you hold your mom's hand very tightly, you do this to her hand. **(grip it)**

❷ Read each sentence and ask students to supply the correct word to complete the sentence.

- We need more help. Please ____ in our class project. **(participate)**
- Joe and Jill ____ the rungs as they climb the ladder. **(grip)**
- This ____ car does not use much gas. **(modern)**
- Bananas get brown and mushy when they ____. **(decay)**

❸ Read each sentence and ask students to tell which word or words are wrong. Then have them provide the correct word from the week's list.

- Let go of a thick branch to pull yourself up into the tree. **(let go of/grip)**
- Most old-fashioned TVs have flat screens. **(old-fashioned/modern)**
- I don't take part in sports because I'm a good athlete. **(don't take part/participate)**

❹ Read each sentence and ask students to decide if it is true or false. If the sentence is false, instruct students to explain why.

- When vegetables decay, they smell good. **(false; vegetables smell bad when they decay)**
- If you grip a paper bag, you are likely to drop it. **(false; when you grip a paper bag, you hold it tightly)**
- A baby born in 2009 was born in modern times. **(true)**
- A baseball player participates in sports. **(true)**

Answers for page 51: 1. D, 2. J, 3. C, 4. G

Name _____

Week 12
A Word a Day

Review Words: participate • decay • modern • grip

Fill in the bubble next to the correct answer.

1. When something *decays*, what happens to it?
- Ⓐ It freezes.
- Ⓑ It melts.
- Ⓒ It grows.
- Ⓓ It rots.

2. Which sentence uses *gripped* correctly?
- Ⓕ Kerry gripped a small sip of milk.
- Ⓖ Amy gripped the water as she swam.
- Ⓗ Amazed, I gripped my eyes and stared.
- Ⓙ My little brother gripped my hand to keep from falling.

3. What do you do when you *participate* in sports?
- Ⓐ You read about sports in books.
- Ⓑ You watch sporting events on TV.
- Ⓒ You play sports with others.
- Ⓓ You write stories about sports.

4. The *modern* light bulb was invented ___.
- Ⓕ in ancient times
- Ⓖ in the last 20 years
- Ⓗ in the 1850s
- Ⓙ when George Washington was president

Writing

Write about an activity that you would like to participate in. Tell why you want to participate. Use **participate** in your sentence.

_____

_____

Week 13
A Word a Day

abbreviated

adjective

A word that is written in a shortened form is **abbreviated**.

The **abbreviated** form of Texas is TX.

What word does each of these **abbreviated** words stand for?

- Mrs.
- Dr.
- St.
- Ave.
- Mr.

Do you have any **abbreviated** words in your address? What are they?

bargain

noun

A **bargain** is something that costs less than the usual price.

Aunt Emma saves lots of money by finding **bargains** at garage sales.

Which of these are probably **bargains**?

- candy bars for $5 each
- two pairs of pants for the price of one
- a free pair of shoes when you buy two pairs
- movie tickets for half price before 6:00 p.m.
- two dollars extra to split a main course at a restaurant

Tell about a time when you went shopping and found a real **bargain**. Why does it feel good to get something that's a **bargain**?

Week 13
A Word a Day

emotion

noun

An **emotion** is a feeling.

Actors must express every **emotion**, from sadness and disappointment to excitement and joy.

Which words name **emotions**?

- love
- heat
- anger
- fright
- softness

Describe how you act when you feel **emotions** like frustration or anger. How about when you feel excitement or joy? Which **emotions** do you prefer?

hardy

adjective

When something is **hardy**, it can survive in difficult conditions.

The **hardy** cactus can survive in the blistering desert sun.

Which words are similar in meaning to **hardy**?

- tough
- fragile
- strong
- flimsy
- sturdy

Tell about a person, animal, or plant that you think is **hardy**. What experience did it go through that makes you think it's **hardy**?

Review

Week 13
A Word a Day

abbreviated • bargain • emotion • hardy

Write on the board the four words studied this week. Read the words with the class and briefly review their meanings. Then conduct the oral activities below.

1 Tell students that you are going to give them a clue about one of the words for the week. They are to find the word that answers the clue.

- This word describes an animal that can live in a very cold place. **(hardy)**
- If you get one of these, you save money. **(a bargain)**
- This is what you did if you wrote the name of your state using two capital letters. **(abbreviated it)**
- Happiness, anger, and loneliness are examples of these. **(emotions)**

2 Read each sentence and ask students to supply the correct word to complete the sentence.

- Mom got a ___ when she bought this table. It only cost ten dollars. **(bargain)**
- Do you think dogs feel ___ like happiness and sadness? **(emotions)**
- The ___ pioneers survived a long trip across the prairie in a covered wagon. **(hardy)**
- "*A-v-e period*" is an ___ way to write the word *Avenue*. **(abbreviated)**

3 Read each sentence and ask students to tell which word or words are wrong. Then have them provide the correct word from the week's list.

- *NYC* is a longer way to write *New York City*. **(a longer/an abbreviated)**
- Only weak creatures like tortoises can survive in hot, dry deserts. **(weak/hardy)**
- At a price of $10.00, this bicycle is too expensive. **(too expensive/a bargain)**

4 Read each sentence and ask students to decide if it is true or false. If the sentence is false, instruct students to explain why.

- Loneliness is an emotion. **(true)**
- If you paid too much for something, you got a bargain. **(false; you got a bargain if you didn't pay very much)**
- *L.A.* is an abbreviated way to write *Los Angeles*. **(true)**
- Hardy people are sick most of the time. **(false; hardy people are strong and healthy)**

Answers for page 55: 1. C, 2. G, 3. C, 4. F

Week 13
A Word a Day

Name _____

Review Words: abbreviated • bargain • emotion • hardy

Fill in the bubble next to the correct answer.

1. Which is an *abbreviated* name?
   - Ⓐ the United States of America
   - Ⓑ New York City
   - Ⓒ USA
   - Ⓓ North America

2. Which word means the opposite of *hardy*?
   - Ⓕ shy
   - Ⓖ weak
   - Ⓗ pale
   - Ⓙ tiny

3. Which word has about the same meaning as *emotion*?
   - Ⓐ idea
   - Ⓑ sickness
   - Ⓒ feeling
   - Ⓓ message

4. I got a *bargain* when I bought a new T-shirt for ___.
   - Ⓕ three dollars
   - Ⓖ twenty dollars
   - Ⓗ fifty dollars
   - Ⓙ one hundred dollars

Writing

Choose an emotion and tell about a time you felt that way. Use **emotion** in your sentence.

_____

_____

Week 14
A Word a Day

gleam

verb

When something **gleams**, it shines and gives off or reflects light.

The medal hanging around the winner's neck **gleamed** in the sunlight.

Which of these might **gleam**?
- mud
- diamonds
- the sun
- a newly washed car
- dirty dishes

What is something you own—or would like to own—that **gleams**? How do you keep it **gleaming**?

harmony

noun

If you work in complete cooperation with others, you work in **harmony**.

The ballplayers worked in such **harmony** that they easily won the game.

Which words are similar in meaning to **harmony**?
- argument
- agreement
- friendship
- togetherness
- disagreement

Tell about something that you do in **harmony** with your classmates, your family, or a friend. Do you think people are able to get more done when they work in **harmony**?

Week 14
A Word a Day

ideal

adjective

Something that is just perfect is **ideal**.

Our timing was **ideal**. The bus arrived just as we got to the bus stop!

Which statements describe something that is **ideal**?

- Summer is the ideal time to go snowboarding.
- A fish is an ideal pet because it takes very little care.
- The ideal place for that plant is in a sunny window.
- I think it would be ideal if I lost the race.
- A sunny day is ideal for a baseball game.

Tell about your **ideal** vacation. Where would you go, whom would you take, and what would you do there? What would be an **ideal** souvenir to bring home?

jovial

adjective

A **jovial** person is always laughing and in a good mood.

Our **jovial** neighbor always has a funny joke or silly trick for us.

Which words describe a **jovial** person?

- jolly
- angry
- fun-loving
- mean
- cheerful

Tell about someone you know who is **jovial**. What makes him or her a **jovial** person? What is fun about being around that person?

Review

Week 14
A Word a Day

gleam • harmony • ideal • jovial

Write on the board the four words studied this week. Read the words with the class and briefly review their meanings. Then conduct the oral activities below.

1 Tell students that you are going to give them a clue about one of the words for the week. They are to find the word that answers the clue.

- Kitchen sinks do this when they are very clean. **(gleam)**
- This word describes a person who laughs a lot. **(jovial)**
- This word has about the same meaning as *agreement*. **(harmony)**
- This word could describe your new shoes if they are just perfect for you. **(ideal)**

2 Read each sentence and ask students to supply the correct word to complete the sentence.

- My ___ dog is friendly and playful and has soft fur. **(ideal)**
- "Ha, ha, ha!" laughed the ___ young man. **(jovial)**
- These smooth, wet rocks ___ in the sun. **(gleam)**
- Please stop arguing. I want you to play together in ___. **(harmony)**

3 Read each sentence and ask students to tell which word or words are wrong. Then have them provide the correct word from the week's list.

- My best friend and I get along perfectly and play with lots of arguments. **(with lots of arguments/in harmony)**
- After I polish them, my shoes look dull and dirty. **(look dull and dirty/gleam)**
- January is the worst month for snowball fights. **(worst/ideal)**
- My grouchy uncle laughed and patted my shoulder. **(grouchy/jovial)**

4 Read each sentence and ask students to decide if it is true or false. If the sentence is false, instruct students to explain why.

- Jovial people are always in a bad mood. **(false; jovial people are always in a good mood)**
- Fierce wild animals make ideal pets. **(false; fierce wild animals do not make perfect pets)**
- Shiny new cars gleam in the sun. **(true)**
- When two groups live in harmony, they usually don't fight with one another. **(true)**

Answers for page 59: 1. A, 2. H, 3. D, 4. G

Week 14
A Word a Day

Name _____

Review Words: gleam • harmony • ideal • jovial

Fill in the bubble next to the correct answer.

1. Which choice has about the same meaning as *ideal*?
   - Ⓐ perfect
   - Ⓑ pretty good
   - Ⓒ okay
   - Ⓓ pretty bad

2. Which word means the opposite of *jovial*?
   - Ⓕ bored
   - Ⓖ friendly
   - Ⓗ grouchy
   - Ⓙ interested

3. Which word has about the same meaning as *gleam*?
   - Ⓐ soften
   - Ⓑ melt
   - Ⓒ freeze
   - Ⓓ shine

4. Two brothers play together in *harmony*. In other words, they ____.
   - Ⓕ are too different to play together
   - Ⓖ get along as playmates
   - Ⓗ don't like playing together
   - Ⓙ hardly ever play together

Writing

Write about what your ideal bedroom would be like. Use **ideal** in your sentence.

_____

_____

Week 15
A Word a Day

loaf

verb

You **loaf** when you spend time being lazy and doing nothing.

I would rather **loaf** on the weekend than do my chores and yardwork.

Which of the following are actions of someone who likes to **loaf**?

- fixing the sink yourself instead of calling the plumber
- taking a nap outside in a hammock
- sitting in the sun and reading
- working all afternoon in the garden
- spending several hours doing homework

Tell how you like to **loaf**? Do you prefer **loafing** or being active?

nominate

verb

You **nominate** someone when you suggest that he or she would be right for a job or deserves special recognition.

I want to **nominate** Henry to head the party committee because he has lots of good ideas.

Which statements might people make when they **nominate** a person?

- "I think April should do the dishes tonight."
- "Gabe would be the best carnival clown."
- "Don't choose Ricky, because he's always late."
- "Brittany should get the award for Best Reader."
- "Diego doesn't want to be team captain."

Whom would you **nominate** for the award of "Most Helpful Person in the School"? Why?

Week 15
A Word a Day

occupy

verb

You **occupy** a place when you live in it.

> We can **occupy** the house just as soon as they finish painting it.

Which of these could an animal **occupy**?

- a seashell
- a cave
- an umbrella
- a tree
- a trumpet

How long to you think you will **occupy** the place where you live now? How many homes have you **occupied** since you were born?

queasy

adjective

If you feel sick to your stomach, you feel **queasy**.

> The rolling of the boat during the storm made everyone feel **queasy**.

Which of these might make a person feel **queasy**?

- eating too much candy
- riding a roller coaster
- sitting quietly in a chair
- eating food that's too spicy
- going for a walk

Tell about a time when someone you know felt **queasy**. What did he or she do to feel better? What are some things that make you feel **queasy**?

© Evan-Moor Corp. • EMC 2792 • A Word a Day

Review

Week 15
A Word a Day

loaf • nominate • occupy • queasy

Write on the board the four words studied this week. Read the words with the class and briefly review their meanings. Then conduct the oral activities below.

❶ Tell students that you are going to give them a clue about one of the words for the week. They are to find the word that answers the clue.

- You have to do this before you elect someone for a job. (**nominate that person**)

- This word describes how you might feel if you ate too much junk food. (**queasy**)

- You might do this on a Saturday when there is nothing that you have to do. (**loaf**)

- A bird in a nest does this. (**occupies the nest**)

❷ Read each sentence and ask students to supply the correct word to complete the sentence.

- I felt ____ after I ate too much frosting. (**queasy**)

- On weekends, Mom and Dad like to ____ around the house. (**loaf**)

- I ____ Taylor for Reading Club President because I know she will do a good job. (**nominate**)

- The Ramirez twins ____ the same bedroom. (**occupy**)

❸ Read each list of words and phrases. Ask students to supply the word that fits best with each.

- sick to your stomach, about to throw up, nauseous (**queasy**)

- inhabit, live inside, make into a home (**occupy**)

- lounge around, be lazy, do nothing (**loaf**)

- suggest for a job, hope to elect, recommend (**nominate**)

❹ Read each sentence and ask students to decide if it is true or false. If the sentence is false, instruct students to explain why.

- When you loaf, you get a lot of work done. (**false; when you loaf, you don't get anything done**)

- You should nominate someone only if you think that person is right for the job. (**true**)

- Sometimes you throw up after feeling queasy for a while. (**true**)

- You occupy your bicycle. (**false; you don't live in your bicycle.**)

Answers for page 63: 1. B, 2. H, 3. C, 4. J

Week 15
A Word a Day

Name _____

Review Words   loaf • nominate • occupy • queasy

Fill in the bubble next to the correct answer.

1. **When do people usually *loaf*?**
   - Ⓐ when they are working
   - Ⓑ when they feel lazy
   - Ⓒ when they exercise
   - Ⓓ when they play sports

2. **Which words have about the same meaning as *queasy*?**
   - Ⓕ bored and tired
   - Ⓖ sad and lonely
   - Ⓗ sick to your stomach
   - Ⓙ sick with a bad cold

3. **Which of these might a dog *occupy*?**
   - Ⓐ a can of dog food
   - Ⓑ a doggie treat
   - Ⓒ a doghouse
   - Ⓓ a bowl full of water

4. **You *nominate* someone for a job because you think he or she ___.**
   - Ⓕ is not a very good worker
   - Ⓖ does not want to do the job
   - Ⓗ does not know how to do the job
   - Ⓙ is the right person for the job

Writing

Choose an animal and write about the kind of home it occupies. Use **occupy** or **occupies** in your sentence.

_____

_____

Week 16
A Word a Day

tedious

adjective

If something is **tedious**, it is boring and repetitious.

We thought that writing all of our spelling words ten times was **tedious**.

Which words mean about the same thing as **tedious**?
- exciting
- fun
- boring
- dull
- tiresome

What is something you have to do that you think is **tedious**?

advertise

verb

You **advertise** when you give information about something for sale.

My dad had to **advertise** in the paper for a week before he sold our old car.

Which of the following might be **advertised**?
- a sale at a department store
- puppies for sale
- the time you go to bed
- a job at a restaurant
- your favorite flavor of ice cream

How would you **advertise** a bicycle that you had for sale? What would you say?

Week 16
A Word a Day

convince

verb

You **convince** someone when you make him or her think the same way that you do.

I couldn't **convince** my mother to let me stay up late on a school night.

Which of these are examples of trying to **convince** someone?

- telling a teacher that your work will be better if you have another day to finish it
- asking a friend what her favorite color is
- telling your parents why you should be able to sleep over at a friend's house
- asking your sister to leave your room
- telling your parents why you need a bigger allowance

Tell about a time when you **convinced** your parents to change their minds about something.

interview

verb

You **interview** someone when you meet and ask questions in order to find out about the person.

The sports reporter was eager to **interview** the players on the winning team.

Which of these might you do when you **interview** someone?

- laugh
- write a poem
- write notes
- take a nap
- use a tape recorder

If you could **interview** anybody, who would it be? What questions would you ask that person?

Review

Week 16
A Word a Day

tedious • advertise • convince • interview

Write on the board the four words studied this week. Read the words with the class and briefly review their meanings. Then conduct the oral activities below.

❶ Tell students that you are going to give them a clue about one of the words for the week. They are to find the word that answers the clue.

- You do this when you put an ad in the newspaper. **(advertise)**
- To get your mom to let you do something, you might need to do this. **(convince her)**
- You do this when you ask your grandma questions about her life for a school report. **(interview her)**
- This word describes having to wait in a long, long line. **(tedious)**

❷ Read each sentence and ask students to supply the correct word to complete the sentence.

- News reporters ___ famous people on TV. **(interview)**
- How can I ___ you that I am right about this? **(convince)**
- Making my bed every single day is a ___ chore. **(tedious)**
- To tell customers about sales, store owners might ___ in the newspaper. **(advertise)**

❸ Read each list of words and phrases. Ask students to supply the word that fits best with each.

- give good reasons, change someone's mind, persuade **(convince)**
- boring, not fun or interesting, repetitious **(tedious)**
- put an ad in the paper, give facts, tell the public **(advertise)**
- ask questions, find information, talk with a famous person on TV **(interview)**

❹ Read each sentence and ask students to decide if it is true or false. If the sentence is false, instruct students to explain why.

- To convince someone that you are right, you need to give good reasons. **(true)**
- Advertising can help store owners sell things. **(true)**
- Most people love doing tedious chores. **(false; most people don't like doing boring, repetitious chores)**
- A news reporter might interview someone on the radio. **(true)**

Answers for page 67: 1. B, 2. F, 3. D, 4. G

A Word a Day • EMC 2792 • © Evan-Moor Corp.

Week 16
A Word a Day

Name _____

Review Words: tedious • advertise • convince • interview

Fill in the bubble next to the correct answer.

1. **Which means about the same as *convince*?**
   - Ⓐ help
   - Ⓑ talk into
   - Ⓒ bother
   - Ⓓ try

2. **Which word has about the same meaning as *tedious*?**
   - Ⓕ boring
   - Ⓖ painful
   - Ⓗ interesting
   - Ⓙ easy

3. **Which person should *advertise*?**
   - Ⓐ a girl who is playing soccer
   - Ⓑ a man who is cooking dinner
   - Ⓒ a boy who is doing his homework
   - Ⓓ a woman who has found a lost dog

4. **Jack wants to *interview* Jill. Jack wants to ____.**
   - Ⓕ tell Jill a story
   - Ⓖ ask Jill some questions
   - Ⓗ teach Jill how to read
   - Ⓙ play baseball with Jill

Writing

What would be the most tedious job in the world? Write about it. Use **tedious** in your sentence.

_____

_____

Week 17
A Word a Day

hideous

adjective

Something **hideous** is ugly or horrible to look at.

> The monster in the movie was so **hideous** that I had to close my eyes.

Which of these might be **hideous**?

- a rotting jack-o'-lantern
- a rainbow
- a beautiful red rose
- a bad wound
- a vampire mask

What is something **hideous** that you've seen? How did you react?

tremble

verb

When you **tremble**, you shake with fear, excitement, or cold.

> I was so nervous before the race, I started to **tremble**.

In which of these situations might you **tremble**?

- riding the scariest roller coaster at the amusement park
- walking through a snowstorm without a jacket
- writing your name on your homework paper
- talking to your friend on the phone
- going on stage to accept an award

Tell about a time when you **trembled** from fear.
Now tell about a time when you **trembled** from the cold.
What is the difference in those feelings?

Week 17
A Word a Day

volume

noun

The loudness of a sound or noise is its **volume**.

> We always turn down the **volume** on the TV when someone is on the phone.

Which of these have a **volume** control?
- a lamp
- a radio
- a CD player
- a shoe
- a tape recorder

What were you doing the last time someone asked you to turn down the **volume**?

complicated

adjective

If something is **complicated**, it has lots of different parts or is difficult to understand.

> My dad helped me follow the **complicated** directions for building my model car.

Which of these would probably be **complicated**?
- writing your full name
- reading a college math book
- flossing your teeth
- making the plans for a skyscraper
- writing instructions for building a greenhouse

What is something **complicated** that you've tried to do? How did it turn out?

Review

Week 17
A Word a Day

hideous • tremble • volume • complicated

Write on the board the four words studied this week. Read the words with the class and briefly review their meanings. Then conduct the oral activities below.

❶ Tell students that you are going to give them a clue about one of the words for the week. They are to find the word that answers the clue.

- This word means the opposite of *beautiful*. **(hideous)**
- This word describes something that is hard to figure out. **(complicated)**
- On a TV, you can turn this up or down. **(the volume)**
- If you went outside on a cold day without a sweater, you might do this. **(tremble)**

❷ Read each sentence and ask students to supply the correct word to complete the sentence.

- This game is so ____ that it will take time to learn the rules. **(complicated)**
- Please turn down the ____ on the radio so that I can sleep. **(volume)**
- I ____ with excitement as I open my birthday presents. **(tremble)**
- My brother looks ____ in that monster mask. **(hideous)**

❸ Read each sentence and ask students to tell which word or words are wrong. Then have them provide the correct word from the week's list.

- This math problem is so simple that it took me an hour to solve it. **(simple/complicated)**
- I was so scared that I began to stop shaking. **(stop shaking/tremble)**
- "How horrible that looks!" I said when I saw the beautiful sight. **(beautiful/hideous)**

❹ Read each sentence and ask students to decide if it is true or false. If the sentence is false, instruct students to explain why.

- Radios, TVs, and CD players all have volume controls. **(true)**
- If a story is complicated, it is easy to understand. **(false; a complicated story is hard to understand)**
- Most kids want to look hideous on the first day of school. **(false; most kids want to look good on the first day of school)**
- People sometimes tremble when they feel excited. **(true)**

Answers for page 71: 1. C, 2. H, 3. B, 4. G

70

A Word a Day • EMC 2792 • © Evan-Moor Corp.

Name _____

Week 17
A Word a Day

Review Words hideous • tremble • volume • complicated

Fill in the bubble next to the correct answer.

1. Which word has about the same meaning as *volume*?
   - Ⓐ color
   - Ⓑ pattern
   - Ⓒ loudness
   - Ⓓ sweetness

2. Which word has about the same meaning as *hideous*?
   - Ⓕ invisible
   - Ⓖ beautiful
   - Ⓗ horrible
   - Ⓙ confusing

3. Which game is *complicated*?
   - Ⓐ an easy game that anyone can play
   - Ⓑ a game with rules that are difficult to understand
   - Ⓒ a game that three-year-old children play
   - Ⓓ a boring game that no one enjoys

4. When you *tremble*, you shake ____.
   - Ⓕ a rattle to make music
   - Ⓖ with fear, excitement, or cold
   - Ⓗ hands with someone you just met
   - Ⓙ your head "no"

Writing

Write about a hideous imaginary creature. Use **hideous** in your sentence.

_____

_____

Week 18
A Word a Day

predict

verb

When you **predict**, you say what you think will happen in the future.

Weather forecasters use computers to help them **predict** the weather.

Which sentences **predict** something?

- I think I'm going to get an A on my test tomorrow.
- I had scrambled eggs for breakfast yesterday.
- I look at the cover of a book and guess what it's about.
- I woke up late and missed the school bus.
- "I bet it's the mail carrier," said Mom when there was a knock at the door.

Try to **predict** what you'll have for dinner tonight. Tomorrow you can report on whether you **predicted** correctly.

shipshape

adjective

If something is clean, neat, and in order, it's **shipshape**.

I don't get my weekly allowance until my room is **shipshape**.

Which of the following are **shipshape**?

- a library with books neatly organized on shelves
- toys stored nicely in a toy box
- a room with laundry thrown all over the floor
- a kitchen right after a big dinner is cooked
- clothes hung neatly in a closet

How do you help keep your classroom **shipshape**? How about your room at home?

Week 18
A Word a Day

agony

noun

If you're in **agony**, you're experiencing very strong pain.

> I was in **agony** when I fell and broke my arm.

Would you be in **agony** if:

- you were taking a bubble bath?
- a brick fell on your bare foot?
- you were eating an ice-cream cone?
- you got a terrible sunburn?
- you had an awful toothache?

Tell about a time when you were in **agony**. What did you do to feel better?

chitchat

verb

When you **chitchat**, you talk about everyday, unimportant things.

> My mom likes to **chitchat** on the phone with her sister about how her day went.

Which topics might you **chitchat** about?

- today's weather
- a family member's operation
- the color of a new nail polish
- your neighbor's serious car accident
- your brother's new haircut

What are some things you **chitchat** about with your friends?

Review

Week 18
A Word a Day

predict • shipshape • agony • chitchat

Write on the board the four words studied this week. Read the words with the class and briefly review their meanings. Then conduct the oral activities below.

1 Tell students that you are going to give them a clue about one of the words for the week. They are to find the word that answers the clue.

- You tell about the future when you do this. **(predict)**
- This word could describe your closet if it was neat, clean, and tidy. **(shipshape)**
- Friends do this on the phone sometimes. **(chitchat)**
- If you broke your leg, you might experience this. **(agony)**

2 Read each sentence and ask students to supply the correct word to complete the sentence.

- I don't mind having a messy room, but my sister likes hers ____. **(shipshape)**
- I can't ____ who will win the contest, can you? **(predict)**
- Dad was in ____ until he took some medicine for his terrible headache. **(agony)**
- At recess, my friends and I have time to ____. **(chitchat)**

3 Read each sentence and ask students to tell which word or words are wrong. Then have them provide the correct word from the week's list.

- After I spent all day cleaning it, my room looked very messy. **(very messy/shipshape)**
- Sometimes it's fun to talk seriously about silly things. **(talk seriously/chitchat)**
- I was in luck after I slammed my finger in the car door. **(luck/agony)**

4 Read each sentence and ask students to decide if it is true or false. If the sentence is false, instruct students to explain why.

- Friends might chitchat about what happened at a birthday party. **(true)**
- People who are in agony feel fine. **(false; people who are in agony are in great pain)**
- People predict what has happened in the past. **(false; people predict what will happen in the future)**
- A shipshape refrigerator is clean and neatly organized. **(true)**

Answers for page 75: 1. D, 2. F, 3. B, 4. H

Name _____

Week 18
A Word a Day

Review Words — predict • shipshape • agony • chitchat

Fill in the bubble next to the correct answer.

1. What do people *chitchat* about?
- Ⓐ serious ideas
- Ⓑ important decisions
- Ⓒ terrible happenings
- Ⓓ everyday events

2. If you are in *agony*, how do you feel?
- Ⓕ You are in great pain.
- Ⓖ You feel okay, but not great.
- Ⓗ You feel wonderful.
- Ⓙ You feel tired and bored.

3. Which is *shipshape*?
- Ⓐ a closet with dirty clothes on the floor
- Ⓑ clean shelves with neatly stacked dishes on them
- Ⓒ a messy desk with books and papers all over it
- Ⓓ a playroom with toys all over the floor

4. When you *predict* rain, you are saying that ___.
- Ⓕ it rained yesterday
- Ⓖ you wish it would stop raining soon
- Ⓗ you think it will rain sometime soon
- Ⓙ it won't rain

Writing

What might you predict that would have a good chance of happening? Use **predict** in your sentence.

_____

_____

Week 19
A Word a Day

occupation

noun

An **occupation** is a person's job or career.

A firefighter has an exciting and dangerous **occupation**.

Which **occupations** are performed outdoors?

- gardening
- farming
- teaching
- writing
- collecting garbage

What **occupation** would you like to have someday? Why are you interested in it?

consent

noun

Consent is permission to do something.

My parents have to give their written **consent** for me to go on a class field trip.

Would you need your parents' **consent** to:

- spend the night at a friend's house?
- buy ice cream from the ice-cream truck?
- get a drink of water?
- wash your hands?
- stay up later than usual?

What did you ask for the last time you asked your parents for their **consent**? What did they say?

Week 19
A Word a Day

famished

adjective

If you're **famished**, you are very, very hungry.

After I skipped lunch, I was so **famished** that I ate three helpings of everything at dinner.

Would you be **famished** if:

- you ate two peas?
- you ate three helpings of mashed potatoes and gravy?
- you hadn't eaten breakfast or lunch?
- you had a big dinner at a restaurant?
- you had the flu and nothing tasted good to you?

Have you ever felt **famished**? Tell about it and how you felt when you finally ate.

hustle

verb

If you **hustle**, you move very quickly and with lots of energy.

We really have to **hustle** if we want to catch the movie that starts in ten minutes.

Which words describe the way you move when you **hustle**?

- like a snail
- as quick as a wink
- sleepily
- like molasses
- like lightning

Tell about a time when you had to **hustle**. What were you doing?

Review

Week 19
A Word a Day

occupation • consent • famished • hustle

Write on the board the four words studied this week. Read the words with the class and briefly review their meanings. Then conduct the oral activities below.

❶ Tell students that you are going to give them a clue about one of the words for the week. They are to find the word that answers the clue.

- If you want to go somewhere, you will probably have to get this from an adult in your family. **(his or her consent)**
- You need to do this if you want to get somewhere fast. **(hustle)**
- You would feel this way if you didn't eat all day. **(famished)**
- Mine is teaching. **(occupation)**

❷ Read each sentence and ask students to supply the correct word to complete the sentence.

- Being a veterinarian is such a helpful _____. **(occupation)**
- The bus will be here in two minutes. We'd better _____. **(hustle)**
- After the hurricane, rescuers fed some _____ dogs that hadn't eaten for days. **(famished)**
- You may go on the camping trip only if you get your parents' _____. **(consent)**

❸ Read each sentence and ask students to tell which word or words are wrong. Then have them provide the correct word from the week's list.

- Let's eat right now! I'm absolutely full! **(full/famished)**
- Now that I've got my mom's refusal, I can stay up late tonight. **(refusal/consent)**
- Let's walk very slowly or we'll be late! **(walk very slowly/hustle)**

❹ Read each sentence and ask students to decide if it is true or false. If the sentence is false, instruct students to explain why.

- Lounging around doing nothing is an occupation. **(false; an occupation is a job or a career)**
- To sleep over at a friend's house, most kids need their parents' consent. **(true)**
- If someone were famished, he or she would probably feel wonderful. **(false; for most people, being famished is unpleasant)**
- If you have only a few minutes to finish your work, you need to hustle. **(true)**

Answers for page 79: 1. B, 2. H, 3. D, 4. H

Week 19
A Word a Day

Name _____

Review Words occupation • consent • famished • hustle

Fill in the bubble next to the correct answer.

1. Which word has about the same meaning as *occupation*?
   - Ⓐ school
   - Ⓑ job
   - Ⓒ hobby
   - Ⓓ home

2. Which word has about the same meaning as *consent*?
   - Ⓕ happiness
   - Ⓖ sadness
   - Ⓗ permission
   - Ⓙ condition

3. When do people *hustle*?
   - Ⓐ when they are being lazy
   - Ⓑ when they are waiting in line
   - Ⓒ when they are lying in the sun
   - Ⓓ when they are in a big hurry

4. If you were *famished*, you would be very ____.
   - Ⓕ happy
   - Ⓖ friendly
   - Ⓗ hungry
   - Ⓙ grateful

Writing

Write about an occupation that you would <u>not</u> like to have. Explain why. Use **occupation** in your sentence.

_____

_____

© Evan-Moor Corp. • EMC 2792 • A Word a Day

79

Week 20
A Word a Day

villain

noun

The **villain** is an evil or wicked character in a story, movie, or play.

> In old cowboy movies, the **villain** usually wears black, and the hero usually wears white.

Which of these are things a **villain** would do?

- take soup to a sick friend
- lie about something
- help a hurt puppy
- rob a bank
- try to trick somebody

Can you think of a **villain** in a story you have read or heard? What was the **villain** like?

dependable

adjective

Something or someone you can count on is **dependable**.

> The guide dog was a **dependable** helper for the blind teenager.

Which of the following show **dependable** behavior?

- doing the dishes after being asked only once
- always coming right home after baseball practice
- waking up late for school every day
- forgetting to bring homework home from school
- calling to let your parents know if you're going to be late

What are some things you do that show that you are a **dependable** person? What's one thing you could do to become more **dependable**?

Week 20
A Word a Day

journey

noun

A **journey** is a long trip or an adventure.

The **journey** across the Great Plains in covered wagons took a long time.

Which of these are **journeys**?

- a trip around the corner to the grocery store
- a drive across the United States to see Grandma
- walking next door to play with the neighbor
- traveling across the ocean on a ship
- flying to see your cousin who lives in another country

Have you ever gone on a **journey**? Where did you go? Where would you like to go if you could go on a **journey** anywhere?

attempt

verb

If you **attempt** something, you try to do it.

The juggler will **attempt** to juggle six flaming torches.

Which words mean about the same thing as **attempt**?

- try
- fail
- give up
- make an effort
- give it a go

What did you **attempt** that was difficult? What happened?

Review

Week 20
A Word a Day

villain • dependable • journey • attempt

Write on the board the four words studied this week. Read the words with the class and briefly review their meanings. Then conduct the oral activities below.

❶ Tell students that you are going to give them a clue about one of the words for the week. They are to find the word that answers the clue.

- In a fairy tale, this character tries to hurt others. **(the villain)**
- Don't give up! Try to do it. **(attempt)**
- This word describes someone who tries hard not to break promises. **(dependable)**
- If you went on one, you'd be gone for a long time. **(a journey)**

❷ Read each sentence and ask students to supply the correct word to complete the sentence.

- The princess took a ___ to a faraway place. **(journey)**
- An evil ___ stole the princess's white horse. **(villain)**
- Cooking can be dangerous! Please do not ___ to do it without an adult. **(attempt)**
- Our teacher picked a ___ student to return the camera to the office. **(dependable)**

❸ Read each sentence and ask students to tell which word or words are wrong. Then have them provide the correct word from the week's list.

- The wicked hero locked the princess in the castle tower. **(hero/villain)**
- Let's pick someone we can't count on to be class president. **(we can't count on/dependable)**
- If you don't try to learn a new skill, you may succeed. **(don't try/attempt)**

❹ Read each sentence and ask students to decide if it is true or false. If the sentence is false, instruct students to explain why.

- You can complete a journey in about an hour. **(false; a journey is a long trip)**
- Most bosses want dependable workers. **(true)**
- In stories, villains are characters who do bad things. **(true)**
- Attempting to win is the same as trying to win. **(true)**

Answers for page 83: 1. C, 2. F, 3. B, 4. J

Week 20
A Word a Day

Name _____

Review Words villain • dependable • journey • attempt

Fill in the bubble next to the correct answer.

1. Which word has about the same meaning as *attempt*?
   - Ⓐ go
   - Ⓑ stop
   - Ⓒ try
   - Ⓓ help

2. Which word means the opposite of *villain*?
   - Ⓕ hero
   - Ⓖ singer
   - Ⓗ cook
   - Ⓙ helper

3. What are *dependable* people like?
   - Ⓐ They are lazy.
   - Ⓑ You can trust them.
   - Ⓒ They are good artists.
   - Ⓓ They make others laugh.

4. A *journey* is a ___ trip.
   - Ⓕ shopping
   - Ⓖ short
   - Ⓗ weekend
   - Ⓙ long

Writing

Invent a name for a villain in a story. Write about what he or she acts like. Use **villain** in your sentence.

_____

_____

Week 21
A Word a Day

forbid

verb

When you **forbid** something, you tell someone they cannot do it.

Most parents **forbid** their children to eat sweets right before dinner.

If you wanted to **forbid** something, which words would you say?

- "Absolutely not!"
- "By all means."
- "Certainly."
- "No way!"
- "Go right ahead."

Do your parents ever **forbid** you from doing something you want to do? Why?

portion

noun

A **portion** is a part or a share of something.

I ate only one piece of pie, but my brother had two **portions**.

Which of these are **portions**?

- a slice of cake
- a dozen eggs
- a chapter of a book
- an hour in a day
- a bag of sugar

What do you like a large **portion** of?
What do you want only a small **portion** of?

Week 21
A Word a Day

vacant

adjective

When a place is empty, it is **vacant**.

The **vacant** house will be painted before new people move in.

Which of these are **vacant**?

- your house
- a hotel room that no one is using
- a store full of customers
- an empty lot
- an apartment with no one living in it

What does it feel like inside a **vacant** house? How is that different from a house where a family lives?

huddle

verb

When a group of people or animals crowd together, they **huddle**.

The whole family tried to **huddle** under one umbrella when they were caught in the rain.

In which of these situations might people **huddle**?

- to keep warm in a snowstorm
- to march in a line
- to make room for another person in a crowded elevator
- to discuss a secret play during a football game
- to fly a kite on the beach

How does it make you feel to see a group of classmates **huddled** together and whispering? Why do you feel like that?

Review

Week 21
A Word a Day

forbid • portion • vacant • huddle

Write on the board the four words studied this week. Read the words with the class and briefly review their meanings. Then conduct the oral activities below.

❶ Tell students that you are going to give them a clue about one of the words for the week. They are to find the word that answers the clue.

- You get this when you get a slice of pizza. **(a portion)**
- Penguins do this when they crowd together to keep warm. **(huddle)**
- This word describes a room that has nobody in it. **(vacant)**
- When your parents say you may not do something, they do this. **(forbid it)**

❷ Read each sentence and ask students to supply the correct word to complete the sentence.

- I ____ you to chew gum at school. **(forbid)**
- We'll all have to ____ in the tent until the rain stops. **(huddle)**
- Apartment 3A is ____. The people who lived there just moved out. **(vacant)**
- I'd like a small ____ of birthday cake, please. **(portion)**

❸ Read each sentence and ask students to tell which word or words are wrong. Then have them provide the correct word from the week's list.

- Jen is not here today, so her seat is filled. **(filled/vacant)**
- You have not cleaned your room yet, so I allow you to go out and play. **(allow/forbid)**
- To make room for more people, we all spread out in the back of the elevator. **(spread out/huddled)**

❹ Read each sentence and ask students to decide if it is true or false. If the sentence is false, instruct students to explain why.

- People sometimes huddle together to keep warm. **(true)**
- A vacant lot has no buildings or play equipment on it. **(true)**
- If your parents forbid you to go somewhere, you may go. **(false; by forbidding you to go, they are saying that you may *not* go)**
- One portion is the same as the whole pot of spaghetti. **(false; a portion is part of something)**

Answers for page 87: 1. D, 2. F, 3. C, 4. G

Week 21
A Word a Day

Name _____

Review Words: forbid • portion • vacant • huddle

Fill in the bubble next to the correct answer.

1. Which word means the opposite of *vacant*?
   - Ⓐ comfortable
   - Ⓑ messy
   - Ⓒ grassy
   - Ⓓ occupied

2. In which sentence does someone *forbid* someone to do something?
   - Ⓕ "No, you may *not* paint on your bedroom wall."
   - Ⓖ "Maybe I will let you draw on your wall with chalk."
   - Ⓗ "I will probably let you draw on the sidewalk with chalk."
   - Ⓙ "Yes, of course you may draw and paint on art paper."

3. Which sentence tells about some puppies *huddling*?
   - Ⓐ They run around crazily.
   - Ⓑ They whine and yelp loudly.
   - Ⓒ They all sleep close together.
   - Ⓓ They play tug-of-war with a rope.

4. A *portion* of pie is a ___.
   - Ⓕ whole pie
   - Ⓖ piece of pie
   - Ⓗ pie recipe
   - Ⓙ piecrust

Writing

Imagine that you are grown-up. What would you forbid kids to do and why? Use **forbid** in your sentence.

_____

_____

Week 22
A Word a Day

ceremony

noun

A **ceremony** is an event held to mark a special occasion.

> The graduation **ceremony** was held on the lawn outside the school.

Which of these are observed with a **ceremony**?

- a wedding
- a bedtime story
- Grandma and Grandpa's 50th wedding anniversary
- receiving a gold medal at the Olympics
- answering the phone

Tell about a **ceremony** you've attended. What occasion was being celebrated?

definite

adjective

Something that is **definite** is certain or for sure.

> My sister was **definite** about going to the movies, but I hadn't made up my mind.

Which of these are **definite** answers?

- "Yes, let's go right now!"
- "Buy me a ticket for Saturday."
- "I'm not sure; I'll call you back."
- "I'll be there at 3:00 sharp."
- "I'm not sure if I like that; let me take another look."

What is something you feel **definite** about?

Week 22
A Word a Day

ingredients

noun

Ingredients are what you put together to make something else.

> Rick put all the **ingredients** for the cookies into the bowl, and I stirred them.

Which of the following would be **ingredients** for cake?
- flour
- eggs
- sugar
- ground beef
- tomato sauce

What are the **ingredients** for your favorite sandwich? Why does a recipe list **ingredients**?

passenger

noun

A **passenger** rides in a vehicle driven or piloted by another person.

> The pilot had to park the plane before the **passengers** could unbuckle their seat belts.

Which of these should a **passenger** do?
- tickle the driver
- wear a seat belt
- help watch for street signs
- throw things out the window
- let the driver concentrate on driving

What are some vehicles that you have been a **passenger** in? In what type of vehicle have you not been a **passenger**, but would like to be?

Review

Week 22
A Word a Day

ceremony • definite • ingredients • passenger

Write on the board the four words studied this week. Read the words with the class and briefly review their meanings. Then conduct the oral activities below.

1 Tell students that you are going to give them a clue about one of the words for the week. They are to find the word that answers the clue.

- People usually have one when they get married. (**a ceremony**)
- You are one when you ride in someone's car. (**a passenger**)
- This word means the opposite of *unsure*. (**definite**)
- For cake frosting, powdered sugar and butter are two of these. (**ingredients**)

2 Read each sentence and ask students to supply the correct word to complete the sentence.

- One ____ got off the bus at the corner of Solano Avenue and King Boulevard. (**passenger**)
- We have ____ plans to visit you on Sunday at 3:00 in the afternoon. (**definite**)
- Our gymnastics team held a special ____ to honor the gymnasts and coaches. (**ceremony**)
- Do we have the ____ we need to make muffins? (**ingredients**)

3 Read each list of words and phrases. Ask students to supply the word that fits best with each.

- certain, all set, sure to happen (**definite**)
- wedding, graduation, honoring a special occasion (**ceremony**)
- bus rider, in the back seat of a car, on an airplane (**passenger**)
- recipe, baking, mix together (**ingredients**)

4 Read each sentence and ask students to decide if it is true or false. If the sentence is false, instruct students to explain why.

- Setting a date and time to do something means that you have definite plans to do it. (**true**)
- A bus passenger rides the bus but does not drive it. (**true**)
- If you are a wedding guest, it is fine to chitchat and make jokes during the ceremony. (**false; a ceremony is an important, formal event**)
- Milk and ice cream are milkshake ingredients. (**true**)

Answers for page 91: 1. B, 2. J, 3. A, 4. G

Name _____

Week 22
A Word a Day

Review Words ceremony • definite • ingredients • passenger

Fill in the bubble next to the correct answer.

1. **Which sentence tells about *ingredients*?**
   - Ⓐ Four quarters or ten dimes equal one dollar.
   - Ⓑ Pancake batter has flour, milk, eggs, and oil in it.
   - Ⓒ The puppies are black with brown paws and tails.
   - Ⓓ I like to eat pancakes on Saturday mornings.

2. **If you have *definite* plans to go somewhere, which is true?**
   - Ⓕ You are not planning to go there.
   - Ⓖ You probably won't go there, but who knows?
   - Ⓗ You'd like to go, but you aren't sure if you can.
   - Ⓙ You have set a certain date and time to go.

3. **Which sentence tells about a *passenger*?**
   - Ⓐ My grandpa takes the bus to work.
   - Ⓑ My mom drives herself to work on the freeway.
   - Ⓒ A pilot lands her plane on the runway.
   - Ⓓ I walk my dog in the park every day.

4. **At a school graduation *ceremony*, people ___.**
   - Ⓕ vote to elect a school president
   - Ⓖ honor the students who are graduating
   - Ⓗ decide which high school they want to go to
   - Ⓙ take tests to see if they are ready to graduate

Writing

Write about the ingredients in something you know how to cook. Use **ingredients** in your sentence.

_____

_____

Week 23
A Word a Day

abandon

verb

When you **abandon** something, you leave it or give it up forever.

The pioneer family had to **abandon** its covered wagon when two of the wooden wheels broke.

Which words mean about the same thing as **abandon**?

- leave behind
- hang on to
- let go of
- keep
- dump

Tell about something you had to **abandon** (a toy, a project, a house) and how you felt about it.

combine

verb

You **combine** things when you put two or more together.

You **combine** sugar, flour, butter, and eggs to make cookie dough.

What color do you get when you **combine** each of these colors?

- red and blue
- black and white
- yellow and blue
- red and white
- red and yellow

What do you like to **combine** to make an ice-cream sundae?

Week 23
A Word a Day

harmless

adjective

Something is **harmless** if it's safe and causes no harm or injury.

> We thought the snake was poisonous, but it turned out to be **harmless**.

Which of the following activities are **harmless**?

- brushing your hair
- jogging on the freeway
- talking to a friend on the phone
- putting on your pajamas
- being shot out of a cannon at the circus

Why would you choose to do a **harmless** activity?
Tell about something you like to do that's **harmless**.

habit

noun

A **habit** is the usual way you act or do things.

> Doing your homework at the same time every day is a good **habit** to get into!

Which of these are good **habits**?

- eating sweets before going to bed
- looking both ways before crossing the street
- getting to school late every day
- saying please and thank you
- making your bed every morning

What is one good **habit** you have at home?
What is a bad **habit** that you'd like to change?

Review

Week 23
A Word a Day

abandon • combine • harmless • habit

Write on the board the four words studied this week. Read the words with the class and briefly review their meanings. Then conduct the oral activities below.

1 Tell students that you are going to give them a clue about one of the words for the week. They are to find the word that answers the clue.

- If you do this with red and yellow paints, you can make orange paint. **(combine them)**
- Biting your fingernails is a bad one. **(habit)**
- This word would not describe a dog that bites. **(harmless)**
- People do this if they have to move out of an unsafe building. **(abandon it)**

2 Read each sentence and ask students to supply the correct word to complete the sentence.

- We had to ___ our vacation plans when Mom couldn't get time off work. **(abandon)**
- Getting to school on time is a good ___ to get into. **(habit)**
- Don't be afraid of our old dog. She is ___. **(harmless)**
- If you ___ sugar and cinnamon, you will have a treat to sprinkle on buttered toast. **(combine)**

3 Read each sentence and ask students to tell which word or words are wrong. Then have them provide the correct word from the week's list.

- It is terrible to move away and rescue your dog in the backyard. **(rescue/abandon)**
- That lizard is dangerous—go ahead and handle it if you like. **(dangerous/harmless)**
- To make the color pink, you split up red and white. **(split up/combine)**

4 Read each sentence and ask students to decide if it is true or false. If the sentence is false, instruct students to explain why.

- Eating a lot of junk food every day is a bad habit. **(true)**
- All wild animals are harmless to humans. **(false; many wild animals can hurt people)**
- When you abandon a plan, you give up on it. **(true)**
- If you combine red and blue paint, you put them in separate jars. **(false; when you combine things, you put them together)**

Answers for page 95: 1. B, 2. J, 3. A, 4. J

Week 23
A Word a Day

Name _____

Review Words abandon • combine • harmless • habit

Fill in the bubble next to the correct answer.

1. **Two-year-old Ana has a *habit* of ___.**
   - Ⓐ starting preschool next year
   - Ⓑ sucking her thumb
   - Ⓒ winning spelling contests
   - Ⓓ turning three in May

2. **Which sentence tells you to *combine* things?**
   - Ⓕ Please don't let the cat out—he may run away.
   - Ⓖ Wake up, get dressed, eat breakfast, and brush your teeth.
   - Ⓗ Paint the living room blue, and paint the kitchen pink.
   - Ⓙ Mix together some flour, baking powder, milk, and eggs.

3. **Which sentence tells about people who *abandoned* a cat?**
   - Ⓐ They just moved away and left the cat by itself.
   - Ⓑ They took the cat to the vet whenever it got sick.
   - Ⓒ They carefully trimmed the cat's long, sharp claws.
   - Ⓓ They fed the cat twice a day and gave it fresh water.

4. **A *harmless* insect is ___.**
   - Ⓕ dangerous
   - Ⓖ poisonous
   - Ⓗ beautiful to look at
   - Ⓙ not going to hurt you

Writing

Write about foods that would <u>not</u> taste good if you combined them. Use **combine** in your sentence.

_____

_____

© Evan-Moor Corp. • EMC 2792 • A Word a Day

Week 24
A Word a Day

warning

noun

A **warning** is a message that alerts you to danger or to a bad thing that might happen.

We left the building when the fire alarm gave us a loud **warning**.

Which of the following are **warnings**?

- "Be careful crossing the street."
- "Hey, we're both reading the same book!"
- "Watch out for that skateboarder!"
- "Don't step in that puddle!"
- "There's a good TV show on tonight."

What **warning** do you often hear at home? What about at school?

exchange

verb

When you **exchange**, you give something to someone and he or she also gives something to you.

We have a gift **exchange** in our club before the winter holidays.

Which of the following are examples of **exchanging**?

- Ying Mei and Jen gave each other birthday gifts.
- My cousin gave me a new toy.
- My mom took back the broken lamp and got another one.
- Let's trade phone numbers.
- You can't wear my new sweater.

What do you own that you would like to **exchange** for something different? What would you **exchange** it for?

Week 24
A Word a Day

contagious

adjective

Something easily passed or spread to another person is **contagious**.

You're supposed to stay home from school if you have a **contagious** disease such as chicken pox.

Which of the following are **contagious**?

- measles
- a bad cold
- your hair color
- mumps
- freckles

Some people say that laughter is **contagious**. What does that mean? Do you think it's true?

artificial

adjective

Something **artificial** is not real or natural.

Dorthea's **artificial** nails looked real, but we knew they weren't.

Which of the following are **artificial**?

- a silver wig
- a sweater made of 100 percent wool
- an imitation leather couch
- fresh vegetables from the garden
- plastic flowers

Tell about something **artificial** that you like.
Tell about something **artificial** that you don't like.

© Evan-Moor Corp. • EMC 2792 • A Word a Day

Review

Week 24
A Word a Day

warning • exchange • contagious • artificial

Write on the board the four words studied this week. Read the words with the class and briefly review their meanings. Then conduct the oral activities below.

1 Tell students that you are going to give them a clue about one of the words for the week. They are to find the word that answers the clue.

- This word means the opposite of *real*. **(artificial)**
- This word describes diseases such as colds and flu. **(contagious)**
- "Watch out!" is one. **(a warning)**
- If you buy a shirt that is too small, you take it back to the store and do this with it. **(exchange it)**

2 Read each sentence and ask students to supply the correct word to complete the sentence.

- My parents often ____ e-mails with their friends. **(exchange)**
- Don't sneeze or cough near other people if your cold is ____. **(contagious)**
- I listened to Mom's ____ and did not pet the strange dog. **(warning)**
- This bright pink cake frosting has ____ coloring in it. **(artificial)**

3 Read each sentence and ask students to tell which word is wrong. Then have them provide the correct word from the week's list.

- Diet sodas have real sugar in them. **(real/artificial)**
- Stay away from me! I have a harmless sickness that you might catch. **(harmless/contagious)**
- A welcome sign on the fence said "Dangerous area! Keep out!" **(welcome/warning)**

4 Read each sentence and ask students to decide if it is true or false. If the sentence is false, instruct students to explain why.

- Most bad colds are contagious. **(true)**
- Some foods have artificial flavors in them. **(true)**
- "Beware of the dog" is a warning. **(true)**
- On your birthday, you exchange gifts with your friends. **(false; the birthday person does not give gifts to others)**

Answers for page 99: 1. A, 2. G, 3. C, 4. H

Week 24
A Word a Day

Name _____

Review Words   warning • exchange • contagious • artificial

Fill in the bubble next to the correct answer.

1. We can talk to each other if we *exchange* ___.
    - Ⓐ phone numbers
    - Ⓑ lunches
    - Ⓒ pencils
    - Ⓓ secret codes

2. Which sentence gives a *warning*?
    - Ⓕ Please feed the cat—he seems hungry.
    - Ⓖ Be careful—that cat sometimes scratches people.
    - Ⓗ Look how cute the kitten looks—he's sleeping in my hat.
    - Ⓙ Cats make good companions for many people.

3. Which word means the opposite of *artificial*?
    - Ⓐ ugly
    - Ⓑ unhealthy
    - Ⓒ natural
    - Ⓓ smart

4. A *contagious* disease ___.
    - Ⓕ does not make people sick
    - Ⓖ is completely harmless
    - Ⓗ can spread from person to person
    - Ⓙ helps sick people to get well

Writing

If you could exchange letters, cards, or e-mails with anyone in the world, who would that person be? Why? Use **exchange** in your sentence.

_____

_____

Week 25
A Word a Day

errand

noun

An **errand** is a short trip to deliver or pick up something.

> I went with my mom on her **errands** to the store, the library, and the gas station.

Which of the following are **errands**?

- returning a book to the classroom next door
- having a picnic in the park
- getting new tires on the car
- buying groceries at the supermarket
- spending a relaxing day at the swimming pool

What was the last **errand** you went on with someone? Do you like going on **errands**? Why or why not?

furious

adjective

If you are **furious**, you're extremely angry.

> My mom was **furious** when our dog dug up her favorite rosebush.

Which of these might make someone **furious**?

- winning a prize
- having a purse stolen
- getting a birthday present
- spilling red paint on a white carpet
- getting a new car

Tell about a time when you were **furious** or when someone was **furious** with you.

Week 25

A Word a Day

doodle

verb

When you **doodle**, you draw or scribble while thinking about something else.

I like to **doodle** squiggly lines on bright paper when I'm listening to music.

Which of these are **doodles**?

- circles drawn down the edge of your math paper
- a painting of mountains, trees, and a rainbow
- a zigzag design on a piece of notepaper
- a drawing of you and your family
- a heart with an arrow through it written on a math paper

Do you **doodle**? If so, when? When you **doodle**, what do you make?

variety

noun

There is **variety** when there are many different items to choose from.

My mom buys a package with a **variety** of small cereal boxes so that I can eat a different cereal every day.

Which of these have **variety**?

- a case of grape juice
- a box of 64 different-colored crayons
- a package of white paper
- a bag of mixed nuts
- an ice-cream store with over 30 flavors of ice cream

Do you like just one flavor of jelly beans, or do you prefer a **variety**?

© Evan-Moor Corp. • EMC 2792 • A Word a Day

101

Review

Week 25
A Word a Day

errand • furious • doodle • variety

Write on the board the four words studied this week. Read the words with the class and briefly review their meanings. Then conduct the oral activities below.

❶ Tell students that you are going to give them a clue about one of the words for the week. They are to find the word that answers the clue.

- Going to the bank to get cash is an example of one. **(an errand)**
- You'd probably feel this way if someone broke your favorite toy on purpose. **(furious)**
- This word means the opposite of *only one kind*. **(variety)**
- You do this if you draw patterns or squiggles while you're talking on the phone. **(doodle)**

❷ Read each sentence and ask students to supply the correct word to complete the sentence.

- I have only one more ___ to run: I need to buy milk. **(errand)**
- It makes my aunt ___ when people harm animals. **(furious)**
- Dad likes to ___ while he's listening to music. **(doodle)**
- I like a ___ of fruit, but Peter only likes bananas. **(variety)**

❸ Read each sentence and ask students to tell which word or words are wrong. Then have them provide the correct word from the week's list.

- Mom went on a long journey to pick up some eggs. **(a long journey/an errand)**
- A rainbow has only one color. **(only one color/a variety of colors)**
- I felt calm and loving after someone stole my bike. **(calm and loving/furious)**

❹ Read each sentence and ask students to decide if it is true or false. If the sentence is false, instruct students to explain why.

- When people doodle, they concentrate on their drawings. **(false; they think about other things while they draw)**
- A supermarket sells a large variety of foods. **(true)**
- Going to buy a birthday card for a friend can be an errand. **(true)**
- When people are furious, they usually smile, laugh, and sing. **(false; people who are furious feel very angry, so they frown and yell)**

Answers for page 103: 1. D, 2. J, 3. C, 4. H

Week 25
A Word a Day

Name _____

Review Words: errand • furious • doodle • variety

Fill in the bubble next to the correct answer.

1. There is a *variety* of fruit in this bowl. There are ___ in it.
   - Ⓐ five green apples
   - Ⓑ two juicy oranges
   - Ⓒ about eight bananas
   - Ⓓ grapes, pears, and apples

2. Which sentence tells about an *errand*?
   - Ⓕ Our whole family took a wonderful vacation.
   - Ⓖ The princess took a long journey to a far-off land.
   - Ⓗ Mom stayed home and fixed the broken water pipe.
   - Ⓙ Dad went to the store to buy a few things for dinner.

3. How does someone feel when he or she is *furious*?
   - Ⓐ calm and happy
   - Ⓑ tired and bored
   - Ⓒ terribly angry
   - Ⓓ very confused

4. When people *doodle*, they ___.
   - Ⓕ try to win drawing contests
   - Ⓖ pay close attention to their artwork
   - Ⓗ draw while thinking about something else
   - Ⓙ try to make pictures that they can give as gifts

Writing

Write about the variety of books in a library. Use **variety** in your sentence.

_____

_____

© Evan-Moor Corp. • EMC 2792 • A Word a Day

Week 26
A Word a Day

enormous

adjective

If something is **enormous**, it's extremely large.

> I thought bears were big, but the dinosaur at the museum was **enormous**!

Which of the following could be described as **enormous**?

- a skyscraper
- an elephant
- a spider
- a whale
- a peanut

What is the most **enormous** thing you've ever seen? Describe it.

shriek

verb

When you **shriek**, you let out a loud, high-pitched scream.

> When my mom saw that mouse, she let out a **shriek** that scared even me!

Which of these might make a person **shriek**?

- riding the world's fastest roller coaster
- painting a pretty picture
- stepping barefoot on a slug
- reading a book
- getting hit from behind with a snowball

Tell about a time when you heard someone **shriek**, or when you let out a **shriek**.

Week 26
A Word a Day

pastry

noun

A sweet baked good made from dough is called a **pastry**.

The bakery smelled delicious early in the morning after the pastries were baked.

Which of these would you find in the **pastry** section of a supermarket?

- apple pie
- hamburger
- cinnamon roll
- strawberry tart
- salad

What's your favorite **pastry**? Do you buy it at a store or bakery, or make it at home?

recite

verb

If you **recite** something, you say it aloud from memory.

Our class learned a poem by heart to recite at the school assembly.

Which ones might you learn to **recite**?

- the alphabet
- a page from the phone book
- the words to a song
- a nursery rhyme
- all the words in a dictionary

What rhyme or song can you **recite**? **Recite** it to a partner or to the class.

Review

Week 26
A Word a Day

enormous • shriek • pastry • recite

Write on the board the four words studied this week. Read the words with the class and briefly review their meanings. Then conduct the oral activities below.

❶ Tell students that you are going to give them a clue about one of the words for the week. They are to find the word that answers the clue.

- If all of a sudden you saw a huge bug, you might do this. **(shriek)**
- Most people love to eat pie, which is this kind of food. **(pastry)**
- You must memorize something before you do this. **(recite it)**
- A human being looks this way to an ant. **(enormous)**

❷ Read each sentence and ask students to supply the correct word to complete the sentence.

- Can you ____ any nursery rhymes? **(recite)**
- My favorite ____ is a cinnamon bun. **(pastry)**
- My jokes are so funny that listeners sometimes ____ with laughter. **(shriek)**
- A blue whale is an absolutely ____ creature. **(enormous)**

❸ Read each sentence and ask students to tell which word or words are wrong. Then have them provide the correct word from the week's list.

- When Marcy saw the snake, she let out a loud whisper. **(whisper/shriek)**
- If you stand next to an elephant, you can tell how tiny it is. **(tiny/enormous)**
- First memorize the poem. Then silently read it for the class. **(silently read/recite)**

❹ Read each sentence and ask students to decide if it is true or false. If the sentence is false, instruct students to explain why.

- Pies are a kind of pastry. **(true)**
- A castle is an enormous building. **(true)**
- A shriek is a soft, low whistle. **(false; a shriek is a loud, high-pitched scream)**
- You can recite a poem without memorizing it first. **(false; when you recite a poem, you say it aloud from memory)**

Answers for page 107: 1. D, 2. J, 3. C, 4. H

Week 26
A Word a Day

Name _____

Review Words enormous • shriek • pastry • recite

Fill in the bubble next to the correct answer.

1. **The movie star lived in an *enormous* house with ___ in it.**
   - Ⓐ one room
   - Ⓑ two rooms
   - Ⓒ three rooms
   - Ⓓ thirty rooms

2. **Which of these foods is a *pastry*?**
   - Ⓕ a bowl of soup
   - Ⓖ a chocolate milkshake
   - Ⓗ a bowl of pudding
   - Ⓙ a cherry tart

3. **Someone is most likely to *shriek* when ___.**
   - Ⓐ he feels bored and tired
   - Ⓑ she feels calm and happy
   - Ⓒ something scary happens suddenly
   - Ⓓ she is putting together a complicated puzzle

4. **When a child *recites* the alphabet, she ___.**
   - Ⓕ reads about it in a book
   - Ⓖ says it silently to herself
   - Ⓗ says it aloud from memory
   - Ⓙ writes it down on a piece of paper

Writing

Think up a new kind of pastry. What does it smell, taste, and look like? Use **pastry** in your sentence.

_____

_____

© Evan-Moor Corp. • EMC 2792 • A Word a Day

Week 27
A Word a Day

antics

noun

Antics are funny or silly actions.

> We loved watching the clowns' **antics** when they squirted water at each other.

Which of the following are **antics**?

- Mom sewing a Halloween costume
- a puppy chasing its tail
- Grandpa taking a nap in his chair
- monkeys swinging through the trees
- children having a pillow fight at a slumber party

What are some of the **antics** you enjoy with your friends?

imitate

verb

You **imitate** when you copy something or someone.

> Grace tried to **imitate** her sister by dressing like her.

Would you **imitate** if you:

- tied your shoelaces in a double knot?
- made your voice sound like a cartoon character?
- wrote your name on your homework?
- made the same gestures as your teacher when you sing in class?
- got a haircut just like your best friend's?

What animal can you **imitate**? Share your **imitation** with the class.

Week 27
A Word a Day

lagoon

noun

A **lagoon** is a small area of shallow water near a larger body of water.

> Water from the ocean reached the **lagoon** at high tide.

Which of these might you find in a **lagoon**?
- lily pads
- fish
- cars
- ducks
- surfers

Would you feel more comfortable swimming in a **lagoon** or in the ocean? Why?

original

adjective

Something is **original** if it is the first of its kind.

> The inventor became famous for all his **original** ideas for new machines.

Which of these would be **original**?
- a glass of water
- a new food dish made by mixing together several ingredients
- greeting cards with designs created by you
- a poem you wrote for your dad's birthday
- the actual glass slipper that Cinderella wore to the ball

Tell about an **original** idea you have had (for a game, a drawing, something you wrote). What made it **original**?

Review

Week 27
A Word a Day

antics • imitate • lagoon • original

Write on the board the four words studied this week. Read the words with the class and briefly review their meanings. Then conduct the oral activities below.

1 Tell students that you are going to give them a clue about one of the words for the week. They are to find the word that answers the clue.

- These actions often make people laugh. **(antics)**
- This word describes something new that someone invents or creates. **(original)**
- This might have fish and ducks in it. **(a lagoon)**
- This word has about the same meaning as *copy*. **(imitate)**

2 Read each sentence and ask students to supply the correct word to complete the sentence.

- Danny can ____ a few different birdcalls. **(imitate)**
- Your painting is truly ____. I have never before seen colors and patterns like yours. **(original)**
- Zoo visitors laughed as they watched the monkeys' ____. **(antics)**
- There is a beautiful blue ____ near the ocean's edge. **(lagoon)**

3 Read each list of words and phrases. Ask students to supply the word that fits best with each.

- coastal pond, body of water, near an ocean **(lagoon)**
- new, creative, first of its kind **(original)**
- copy, act the same, try to be like **(imitate)**
- clowning around, being silly, funny actions **(antics)**

4 Read each sentence and ask students to decide if it is true or false. If the sentence is false, instruct students to explain why.

- If you copy someone else's painting, your painting is not original. **(true)**
- Some comedians imitate famous people. **(true)**
- A lagoon is larger than an ocean. **(false; a lagoon is a small body of water, and an ocean is a large body of water)**
- Antics make most people feel sad. **(false; antics are funny or silly actions that make people laugh)**

Answers for page 111: 1. B, 2. H, 3. B, 4. F

Name _____

Week 27
A Word a Day

Review Words antics • imitate • lagoon • original

Fill in the bubble next to the correct answer.

1. **What can people do in a *lagoon*?**
   - Ⓐ sail enormous ships
   - Ⓑ swim around
   - Ⓒ have friends over for dinner
   - Ⓓ ride bikes

2. **You *imitate* someone's voice when you ___.**
   - Ⓕ listen to the person speak
   - Ⓖ wish you had a voice like that
   - Ⓗ make your voice sound like his or hers
   - Ⓙ ask that person to speak more clearly

3. **We had fun watching the ___ *antics*.**
   - Ⓐ building's
   - Ⓑ kitten's
   - Ⓒ garden's
   - Ⓓ principal's

4. **The singer recorded an *original* song that ___.**
   - Ⓕ she wrote herself
   - Ⓖ someone wrote long ago
   - Ⓗ she heard when she was a child
   - Ⓙ a band played 20 years ago

Writing

Whose voice do you wish you could imitate? Why? Use **imitate** in your sentence.

_____

_____

Week 28
A Word a Day

prevent

verb

If you keep something from happening, you **prevent** it.

We can **prevent** some diseases by giving people vaccinations.

Which of the following can people sometimes **prevent**?

- a thunderstorm
- forest fires
- illness
- automobile accidents
- the sun rising

Tell about something your parents or teacher **prevented** you from doing. What were their reasons? How did you feel?

available

adjective

If something is ready to be used, it is **available**.

My mom asked Jenny if she was **available** to baby-sit on Friday night.

Which of the following let you know that something is **available**?

- "The doctor can see you now."
- "The tacos you ordered are ready."
- "We won't have that book in the store until next week."
- "I'm sorry; we don't have that sweater in your size right now."
- "Tickets are on sale now for next week's concert."

Tell about a time you wanted something that wasn't **available**. What did you do?

Week 28
A Word a Day

estimate

verb

When you **estimate**, you make a guess based on what you know.

> There are too many jelly beans to count; let's try to **estimate** the number.

Which of these might you need to **estimate**?

- the number of eggs in a dozen
- the amount of water needed by a plant
- the number of people in your family
- the number of people born each day on Earth
- the number of tomatoes needed to make a quart of salsa

How could you make a good **estimate** of the number of people in this school?

cozy

adjective

Something that feels warm, comfortable, and snug is **cozy**.

> My **cozy** slippers keep my feet warm on cold winter nights.

Which of these are **cozy**?

- a quilt
- a sweater that makes you itch
- a purring kitten curled up in your lap
- flannel pajamas on a chilly night
- a bathing suit

What are your favorite things to help you feel **cozy**?

Review

Week 28
A Word a Day

prevent • available • estimate • cozy

Write on the board the four words studied this week. Read the words with the class and briefly review their meanings. Then conduct the oral activities below.

1 Tell students that you are going to give them a clue about one of the words for the week. They are to find the word that answers the clue.

- When it is cold outside, a thick, soft blanket feels this way. **(cozy)**
- You do this when you make a close guess. **(estimate)**
- This word describes something that is possible to get or use. **(available)**
- This word means the opposite of *allow*. **(prevent)**

2 Read each sentence and ask students to supply the correct word to complete the sentence.

- All winter, the bear slept in its ____ den. **(cozy)**
- If you are ____ next weekend, let's play soccer. **(available)**
- To ____ cavities, brush your teeth twice a day. **(prevent)**
- I ____ that over 200 people are here at the game. **(estimate)**

3 Read each sentence and ask students to tell which word or words are wrong. Then have them provide the correct word from the week's list.

- Start forest fires—make sure campfires are out before you go to sleep! **(Start/Prevent)**
- Shelby can definitely baby-sit for us. She said she will be busy all weekend. **(busy/available)**
- Count the number of fish in the ocean. **(Count/Estimate)**
- My dog loves her uncomfortable bed. **(uncomfortable/cozy)**

4 Read each sentence and ask students to decide if it is true or false. If the sentence is false, instruct students to explain why.

- When you estimate, you find an exact number. **(false; you make a close guess)**
- Sunscreen helps to prevent sunburns. **(true)**
- Cozy rooms are cold and uncomfortable. **(false; they are warm and comfortable)**
- If tickets are available, there are still some left. **(true)**

Answers for page 115: 1. A, 2. G, 3. C, 4. J

Name _____

Week 28
A Word a Day

Review Words prevent • available • estimate • cozy

Fill in the bubble next to the correct answer.

1. **Which word has about the same meaning as *estimate*?**
   - Ⓐ guess
   - Ⓑ ask
   - Ⓒ choose
   - Ⓓ know

2. **You might *prevent* an accident by ___.**
   - Ⓕ getting badly hurt
   - Ⓖ following safety rules
   - Ⓗ leaving toys on stairs
   - Ⓙ stepping on a bee

3. **Which word means the opposite of *cozy*?**
   - Ⓐ dark
   - Ⓑ unhealthy
   - Ⓒ uncomfortable
   - Ⓓ enormous

4. **When you are *available* to help a friend, you are ___.**
   - Ⓕ unable to help her
   - Ⓖ not ready to help her
   - Ⓗ too selfish to help her
   - Ⓙ ready and able to help her

Writing

Write about a cozy room. This might be a real room or an imaginary room. Use **cozy** in your sentence.

_____

_____

Week 29
A Word a Day

clumsy

adjective

Someone or something that moves in an awkward, ungraceful way is **clumsy**.

I felt so **clumsy** when I tripped over my shoelace and dropped my lunch tray.

Would you feel **clumsy** if you:

- spilled your glass of juice?
- tripped over the curb and fell?
- won a dance contest?
- walked on a high wire without falling?
- stepped on your dance partner's toes?

Tell about a time when you did something that made you feel **clumsy**. What did you do?

shelter

noun

A **shelter** is a safe place to stay.

When it started raining, we found **shelter** in a nearby store to keep dry.

Which of these could be **shelters**?

- a cave
- a playground
- a park
- a treehouse
- a barn

If you were lost in the woods, what could you use to make a **shelter** for spending the night?

Week 29
A Word a Day

donate

verb

You **donate** when you give your time, money, or things to help others.

We will **donate** the money we earn from collecting cans to help feed homeless children.

Which words mean about the same thing as **donate**?

- offer
- keep
- share
- protect
- contribute

What is something you own that you could **donate** to help a person in need?

swarm

noun

A **swarm** is a large number of insects, animals, or people that move together as a group.

We had to stay inside because a **swarm** of bees had just left its hive.

Which of these are **swarms**?

- a duck in a pond
- a group of people following a parade
- a child playing in the park
- an army of ants moving through the rainforest
- a mass of mosquitoes buzzing around a campground

Have you ever seen or been around a **swarm** of people or insects? Describe what it was like.

Review

Week 29
A Word a Day

clumsy • shelter • donate • swarm

Write on the board the four words studied this week. Read the words with the class and briefly review their meanings. Then conduct the oral activities below.

1 Tell students that you are going to give them a clue about one of the words for the week. They are to find the word that answers the clue.

- You need this when it rains or snows. **(a shelter)**
- You could do this with clothes, toys, or books that you don't want to keep. **(donate them)**
- This is a name for a big group of mosquitoes that fly around together. **(a swarm)**
- This word describes someone who keeps accidentally dropping things. **(clumsy)**

2 Read each sentence and ask students to supply the correct word to complete the sentence.

- Our ___ puppy tripped over her own big feet. **(clumsy)**
- A ___ of flies hovered over the garbage cans. **(swarm)**
- Mom and Dad ___ their time to help clean up parks. **(donate)**
- Rabbits have underground ___ called "burrows." **(shelters)**

3 Read each sentence and ask students to tell which word is wrong. Then have them provide the correct word from the week's list.

- That graceful girl bumped into me twice. **(graceful/clumsy)**
- When a bear knocked over the hive, a pair of angry bees flew out and stung it. **(pair/swarm)**
- To help homeless children, I'm going to keep some of my toys. **(keep/donate)**

4 Read each sentence and ask students to decide if it is true or false. If the sentence is false, instruct students to explain why.

- A shelter can keep you warm, safe, and dry. **(true)**
- There are about three or four mosquitoes in a swarm. **(false; a swarm has a large number of mosquitoes in it)**
- You can donate money, time, or toys to help others. **(true)**
- Most ballet dancers are clumsy. **(false; most ballet dancers are graceful)**

Answers for page 119: 1. A, 2. G, 3. D, 4. J

Week 29
A Word a Day

Name _____

Review Words: clumsy • shelter • donate • swarm

Fill in the bubble next to the correct answer.

1. **Which word has about the same meaning as *donate*?**
   - Ⓐ give
   - Ⓑ sell
   - Ⓒ buy
   - Ⓓ borrow

2. **A bear might find *shelter* in a ___.**
   - Ⓕ pond
   - Ⓖ cave
   - Ⓗ hotel
   - Ⓙ nest

3. **Which word means the opposite of *clumsy*?**
   - Ⓐ kind
   - Ⓑ intelligent
   - Ⓒ beautiful
   - Ⓓ graceful

4. **There are ___ bees in a *swarm*.**
   - Ⓕ two
   - Ⓖ five
   - Ⓗ very few
   - Ⓙ many

Writing

Imagine that you are building a shelter for you and your friends to play in. What would your shelter be like? Use **shelter** in your sentence.

_____

_____

Week 30
A Word a Day

tempting

adjective

Something that's inviting and hard to resist is **tempting**.

> Although I had work to do, his offer to go to the beach was too **tempting** to pass up.

Which of these might be **tempting**?

- getting stung by a bee
- being offered a piece of chocolate cake
- falling out of a tree and breaking your arm
- having your brother or sister offer to do your chores for you
- being invited to go to a concert when your favorite singing group is performing

Tell about a time when something was so **tempting** that you couldn't pass it up.

accomplishment

noun

An **accomplishment** is something that has been done successfully.

> It was a major **accomplishment** for the blind hiker to reach the top of the mountain peak.

Which of these are **accomplishments**?

- learning to play a difficult piece on the piano
- sitting on the couch watching television
- getting all the words right on a spelling test
- getting a gold medal for winning an Olympic event
- giving up on a math problem after trying to do it once

What is one of your greatest **accomplishments** so far? What other **accomplishments** would you like to achieve in your life?

Week 30
A Word a Day

refuse

verb

If you say no to something, you **refuse** it.

When Martin was asked to baby-sit, he **refused** because he had made other plans.

Which statements could be used to **refuse** something?

- "No, I won't."
- "Sure, I'd love to go."
- "I think I'll just stay home tonight."
- "I'll go to the party with you."
- "Sorry, but I don't eat meat."

Tell about a time when you **refused** to do something. What happened? When is it a good idea to **refuse** to do something? When isn't it such a good idea?

unusual

adjective

If something is strange or different, it's **unusual**.

It was **unusual** for my dad to be home at three o'clock in the afternoon instead of around dinnertime.

Would it be **unusual**:

- to learn to ride a bike?
- to see a two-headed dog?
- to read a book backward?
- to see a clown at the circus?
- for tennis balls to fall from the sky?

Tell about something **unusual** that happened to you or someone you know.

Review

Week 30
A Word a Day

tempting • accomplishment • refuse • unusual

Write on the board the four words studied this week. Read the words with the class and briefly review their meanings. Then conduct the oral activities below.

1 Tell students that you are going to give them a clue about one of the words for the week. They are to find the word that answers the clue.

- This is what you do when you say you won't do something. **(refuse)**
- This word describes being asked to a movie when you are doing homework. **(tempting)**
- Graduating from high school is one. **(an accomplishment)**
- This word could describe a person with pink hair and clothes of many different colors. **(unusual)**

2 Read each sentence and ask students to supply the correct word to complete the sentence.

- Junk food is not good for you, but it can be ___. **(tempting)**
- I've never heard that name before; it's a bit ___. **(unusual)**
- I hope you won't ___ my invitation to dinner. **(refuse)**
- I won the race! I'm so proud of my ___. **(accomplishment)**

3 Read each sentence and ask students to tell which word or words are wrong. Then have them provide the correct word from the week's list.

- I couldn't say yes when I was asked to sit in the cockpit next to the pilot. **(say yes/refuse)**
- It would be normal for it to snow in August in Florida. **(normal/unusual)**
- Learning to play guitar is one of Robyn's many failures. **(failures/accomplishments)**
- That cake looks disgusting, but I'm too full for dessert. **(disgusting/tempting)**

4 Read each sentence and ask students to decide if it is true or false. If the sentence is false, instruct students to explain why.

- Most people feel proud of their accomplishments. **(true)**
- When you are very tired, it is tempting to stay up late. **(false; staying up when you are tired is not inviting at all)**
- A dog is obedient if it refuses to come when you call it. **(false; an obedient dog would come when called)**
- A short-necked giraffe would be unusual. **(true)**

Answers for page 123: 1. B, 2. F, 3. B, 4. J

Name _____

Week 30
A Word a Day

Review Words: tempting • accomplishment • refuse • unusual

Fill in the bubble next to the correct answer.

1. Which words tell about an *accomplishment*?
   - Ⓐ having brown eyes
   - Ⓑ doing well on a test
   - Ⓒ being in second grade
   - Ⓓ smiling at a friend

2. For a dog, it might be *tempting* to ____.
   - Ⓕ grab food from a person's plate
   - Ⓖ sleep outdoors in the rain
   - Ⓗ have nothing to eat for days
   - Ⓙ spend time locked in a cage

3. Which word has about the same meaning as *unusual*?
   - Ⓐ normal
   - Ⓑ strange
   - Ⓒ beautiful
   - Ⓓ hideous

4. I absolutely *refuse* to go. I ____.
   - Ⓕ will definitely go
   - Ⓖ will probably go
   - Ⓗ want to go, but I can't
   - Ⓙ will not go—no way

Writing

Write about an accomplishment of yours. Use **accomplishment** in your sentence.

_____

_____

Week 31
A Word a Day

jiffy

noun

A **jiffy** is a very short amount of time.

When the runner's shoe came untied in the middle of the race, she tied it in a **jiffy**.

Which of these could you do in a **jiffy**?

- clap your hands
- zip up your jacket
- turn on a light switch
- make and decorate a cake
- read a book with ten chapters

What do you do to get ready for school that takes only a **jiffy**? What takes longer than a **jiffy**?

entire

adjective

The **entire** amount is all of it.

It's not a very good idea to eat an **entire** carton of ice cream for dessert.

Which of the following mean about the same thing as **entire**?

- all
- half
- none
- whole
- 100 percent

Is it healthy to eat an **entire** family-sized pizza? Why or why not?

Week 31
A Word a Day

consequence

noun

A **consequence** is what happens as the result of another action.

One **consequence** of not doing homework might be getting a poor grade.

What would be the **consequence** of:
- leaving your bike out in the rain?
- not returning a library book on time?
- not getting enough sleep at night?
- leaving crayons out in the sun?
- leaving a cake in the oven too long?

Tell about a time when there was a bad **consequence** because of something you did. What did you learn?

humorous

adjective

Something funny or amusing is **humorous**.

The cartoon he brought in was so **humorous** that we all laughed.

Which of these are **humorous**?
- a joke
- a cartoon
- a magician
- a scary movie
- a comic book

Tell about something **humorous** that you have seen or read. What was **humorous** about it?

Review

Week 31
A Word a Day

jiffy • entire • consequence • humorous

Write on the board the four words studied this week. Read the words with the class and briefly review their meanings. Then conduct the oral activities below.

❶ Tell students that you are going to give them a clue about one of the words for the week. They are to find the word that answers the clue.

- This is something that happens because of something else. **(a consequence)**
- If you hurry, you can get ready to leave in this amount of time. **(a jiffy)**
- This word describes something that would make you laugh. **(humorous)**
- This word has about the same meaning as *whole*. **(entire)**

❷ Read each sentence and ask students to supply the correct word to complete the sentence.

- I hadn't eaten for an ___ day, so I was really hungry. **(entire)**
- I didn't study my spelling words. As a ___, I didn't do well on the test. **(consequence)**
- I read a ___ book that made me giggle. **(humorous)**
- Please wait for me. I'll be ready to go in a ___. **(jiffy)**

❸ Read each sentence and ask students to tell which word or words are wrong. Then have them provide the correct word from the week's list.

- You won't have to wait long. She'll be here in two years. **(two years/a jiffy)**
- People laughed at the sad sight. **(sad/humorous)**
- I liked this story so much, I read part of the book in just one night. **(part of the/the entire)**

❹ Read each sentence and ask students to decide if it is true or false. If the sentence is false, instruct students to explain why.

- Every action you take is a consequence. **(false; a consequence happens because of an action)**
- Humorous movies are funny. **(true)**
- A jiffy lasts a few hours. **(false; a jiffy is a short period of time)**
- An entire hour is the same as half an hour. **(false; an entire hour is a whole hour, or two half hours)**

Answers for page 127: 1. C, 2. G, 3. D, 4. G

Week 31
A Word a Day

Name _____

Review Words: jiffy • entire • consequence • humorous

Fill in the bubble next to the correct answer.

1. Which word has about the same meaning as *humorous*?
   - Ⓐ interesting
   - Ⓑ strange
   - Ⓒ funny
   - Ⓓ disgusting

2. If it rained for a week, which might be a *consequence*?
   - Ⓕ People's lawns would dry up.
   - Ⓖ There would be puddles everywhere.
   - Ⓗ Students would be quiet in class.
   - Ⓙ Students would be noisy in class.

3. If a man ate an *entire* pizza, how much did he eat?
   - Ⓐ none of it
   - Ⓑ one slice
   - Ⓒ half of it
   - Ⓓ all of it

4. I can ___ in a *jiffy*.
   - Ⓕ take a long journey
   - Ⓖ put on my jacket
   - Ⓗ watch a movie
   - Ⓙ read a book

Writing

Write about an animal you saw doing something humorous. Use **humorous** in your sentence.

_____

_____

Week 32
A Word a Day

sturdy

adjective

Something **sturdy** is strong and solid.

The **sturdy** bookshelf was able to hold the weight of many books.

Which of these are **sturdy**?

- a piano
- a large desk
- a feather
- a dish towel
- a refrigerator

What is something in your house that's **sturdy**? How is this useful?

slither

verb

When something **slithers**, it moves with a gliding motion.

We watched the snake **slither** on its belly up and over the rock.

Which of the following might **slither**?

- an eel
- a bird
- a snail
- a worm
- a rabbit

Tell about an animal that you've seen **slither**. How is this way of moving different from the way other animals move?

Week 32
A Word a Day

physician

noun

A **physician** is a doctor.

The **physician** checked my throat, and then he wrote a prescription for some medicine.

Which of these might a **physician** use?

- a guitar
- a stethoscope
- a thermometer
- a basketball
- an X-ray

Tell about a time when you went to a **physician**. Why did you go and what did he or she do?

assist

verb

When you help someone, you **assist** him or her.

The magician called for a volunteer from the audience to **assist** him with a trick.

Which of the following are offers to **assist** someone?

- "I can tie my shoes all by myself!"
- "Let me help you carry the groceries."
- "I built this model airplane without any help!"
- "I'll come over and help you paint the room."
- "May I show you another way to do this math problem?"

Tell about a time when someone **assisted** you. When did you **assist** someone?

Review

Week 32
A Word a Day

sturdy • slither • physician • assist

Write on the board the four words studied this week. Read the words with the class and briefly review their meanings. Then conduct the oral activities below.

1 Tell students that you are going to give them a clue about one of the words for the week. They are to find the word that answers the clue.

- When you help someone, you do this. **(assist that person)**
- If you were very sick, you would need to see one. **(a physician)**
- Most people would rather have a bicycle that is like this than a bike that is falling apart. **(sturdy)**
- Snakes do this when they move along the ground. **(slither)**

2 Read each sentence and ask students to supply the correct word to complete the sentence.

- Dr. Contreras is a ___ at Children's Hospital. **(physician)**
- You look like you need help. Please let me ___ you. **(assist)**
- Don't use that ladder! It does not look very ___. **(sturdy)**
- I watched a slug ___ across the garden path. **(slither)**

3 Read each list of words and phrases. Ask students to supply the word that fits best with each.

- strong, solid, well-built **(sturdy)**
- help, aid, give someone a hand **(assist)**
- hospital, doctor, medical worker **(physician)**
- slide, slip, glide **(slither)**

4 Read each sentence and ask students to decide if it is true or false. If the sentence is false, instruct students to explain why.

- A pediatrician, a doctor who treats children, is a physician. **(true)**
- To assist your grandmother, you should keep watching television while she washes the dishes. **(false; to assist her, you should help her with the chore)**
- A sturdy box falls apart easily. **(false; a sturdy box is strong and solid)**
- When an elephant walks through the jungle, it slithers. **(false; an elephant does not move with a gliding motion like a snake does)**

Answers for page 131: 1. C, 2. J, 3. D, 4. F

Week 32
A Word a Day

Name _____

Review Words: sturdy • slither • physician • assist

Fill in the bubble next to the correct answer.

1. **Which word means the opposite of *sturdy*?**
   - Ⓐ serious
   - Ⓑ smooth
   - Ⓒ weak
   - Ⓓ lazy

2. **Which word has about the same meaning as *physician*?**
   - Ⓕ teacher
   - Ⓖ soldier
   - Ⓗ lawyer
   - Ⓙ doctor

3. **What does a snake do when it *slithers*?**
   - Ⓐ It eats small animals.
   - Ⓑ It makes a rattling noise.
   - Ⓒ It sleeps on a sunny rock.
   - Ⓓ It slides along on its belly.

4. **I *assist* my little sister by ___.**
   - Ⓕ tying her shoes for her
   - Ⓖ telling her to be quiet
   - Ⓗ ignoring her
   - Ⓙ playing with her toys

Writing

Would you like to be a physician when you grow up? Why or why not? Use **physician** in your sentence.

_____

_____

Week 33
A Word a Day

enthusiastic

adjective

If you're really excited about something, you're **enthusiastic** about it.

The children were so **enthusiastic** about taking a vacation that they packed their suitcases a week early!

Would you be **enthusiastic** about:
- having a cold?
- winning a contest?
- getting a new puppy?
- having to clean the entire house by yourself?
- having a friend spend the night at your house?

Tell about a time when you were really **enthusiastic** about something. What were you **enthusiastic** about? How did you act?

beverage

noun

A **beverage** is something to drink.

The Hawaiian restaurant was famous for its fruit **beverages**.

Which of the following are **beverages**?
- tea
- milk
- pudding
- potato chips
- hot chocolate

Name the **beverage** you usually drink at each meal. What is your favorite **beverage**?

Week 33
A Word a Day

tidy

adjective

A **tidy** place is very neat, with everything in order.

Her room was so **tidy** that she could always find anything she needed.

Which of these words mean about the same thing as **tidy**?

- clean
- sloppy
- orderly
- messy
- organized

Do you like your room to be **tidy**? Why or why not? What do you do to keep your room **tidy**?

detour

noun

A **detour** is a route you can follow when the main route is closed for some reason.

When the main road was being paved, we had to take a **detour** to get to our house.

Which of these situations would require a **detour** to be set up?

- The highway is open for travel.
- There will be a street fair downtown.
- There are stoplights at the intersection.
- The freeway ramp is closed due to an accident.
- A parade is planned down the main street in town.

Tell about a time when you had to take a **detour**. Why did you have to do so? Did you get anxious or confused?

Review

Week 33
A Word a Day

enthusiastic • beverage • tidy • detour

Write on the board the four words studied this week. Read the words with the class and briefly review their meanings. Then conduct the oral activities below.

❶ Tell students that you are going to give them a clue about one of the words for the week. They are to find the word that answers the clue.

- This word describes a room that is neat and well organized. **(tidy)**

- When the main road is closed, a driver may have to take one of these. **(a detour)**

- You drink this. **(a beverage)**

- You feel this way about doing fun activities. **(enthusiastic)**

❷ Read each sentence and ask students to supply the correct word to complete the sentence.

- I don't feel very ___ about getting a flu shot. **(enthusiastic)**

- They closed the highway for repairs, so Dad had to take a ___ to get home. **(detour)**

- Would you like a ___ and something to eat? **(beverage)**

- If you want a ___ bedroom, you will have to put your clothes and toys away. **(tidy)**

❸ Read each sentence and ask students to tell which word or words are wrong. Then have them provide the correct word from the week's list.

- After Mom cleaned my room, it looked nice and messy. **(messy/tidy)**

- The main road was closed, so we took the main road. **(the main road/a detour)**

- "Yay! Let's go!" I yelled in a bored voice. **(a bored/an enthusiastic)**

- Please drink your solid food. **(solid food/beverage)**

❹ Read each sentence and ask students to decide if it is true or false. If the sentence is false, instruct students to explain why.

- Juice is a beverage. **(true)**

- In a tidy room, things are put away where they belong. **(true)**

- A baseball fan feels enthusiastic about baseball. **(true)**

- Taking a detour is the same as driving on the main road. **(false; drivers take detours when main roads are closed)**

Answers for page 135: 1. C, 2. J, 3. B, 4. H

134

A Word a Day • EMC 2792 • © Evan-Moor Corp.

Week 33
A Word a Day

Name _____

Review Words: enthusiastic • beverage • tidy • detour

Fill in the bubble next to the correct answer.

1. Which sounds most *enthusiastic*?
   - Ⓐ "I'll go if you want me to."
   - Ⓑ "No way! I hate that place!"
   - Ⓒ "I'd love to go with you!"
   - Ⓓ "Can't we go home now?"

2. Which of these is a *beverage*?
   - Ⓕ a slice of bread
   - Ⓖ a carrot stick
   - Ⓗ a bowl of stew
   - Ⓙ a glass of milk

3. When a man takes a *detour*, what does he do?
   - Ⓐ He borrows a friend's car because his own car is broken.
   - Ⓑ He goes a different way when the main road is closed.
   - Ⓒ He doesn't drive until workers finish repairing the road.
   - Ⓓ He drives very slowly while workers repair the road.

4. Which word means the opposite of *tidy*?
   - Ⓕ quiet
   - Ⓖ polite
   - Ⓗ messy
   - Ⓙ silly

Writing

What beverage would you order if you went to a restaurant? Use **beverage** in your sentence.

_____

_____

Week 34
A Word a Day

perishable

adjective

Something that can spoil or rot is **perishable**.

> Because meat is **perishable**, we keep it in the cooler when we go camping.

Which of the following are **perishable**?

- fruit
- milk
- chicken
- shampoo
- a box of cereal

What **perishable** foods do you bring in your lunch? How can you keep **perishable** foods fresh until you eat them?

appetite

noun

Your **appetite** is your hunger for food.

> I'm not allowed to have snacks after four o'clock so that I won't spoil my **appetite** for dinner.

Which of the following appeal to your **appetite**?

- rich, dark chocolate cake
- hot buttered popcorn
- strong, black coffee
- tart, crunchy apples
- spicy chili

What kind of food do you have the biggest **appetite** for? How do you satisfy your **appetite**?

Week 34
A Word a Day

audience

noun

An **audience** is a group of people who watch a show or a performance.

The **audience** clapped to let the actors know that they enjoyed the play.

At which of these would you find an **audience**?

- a musical program
- a graduation ceremony
- the grocery store
- your kitchen table
- the movies

Tell about a time when you were a member of an **audience**. What are some polite rules of behavior when you're in an **audience**?

avoid

verb

You **avoid** something if you try to stay away from it or keep it from happening.

Jenny **avoided** me at school because she borrowed my book and forgot to return it.

Which of these would you try to **avoid**?

- getting a birthday present
- a baseball that was going to hit you
- showing your parents an excellent report card
- stepping in a mud puddle if you're wearing sandals
- riding your bike on the sidewalk where a child is playing

If you could **avoid** doing one thing, what would it be and why?

Review

Week 34
A Word a Day

perishable • appetite • audience • avoid

Write on the board the four words studied this week. Read the words with the class and briefly review their meanings. Then conduct the oral activities below.

❶ Tell students that you are going to give them a clue about one of the words for the week. They are to find the word that answers the clue.

- When you are in a play, this group of people watches you perform. **(the audience)**
- This kind of food can rot. **(perishable)**
- If you have a big one of these, you are hungry. **(an appetite)**
- You do this when you don't want to be around a person. **(avoid him or her)**

❷ Read each sentence and ask students to supply the correct word to complete the sentence.

- We all sat in the ____ at my sister's dance performance. **(audience)**
- Please don't ____ me just because we had an argument. Let's get together and talk. **(avoid)**
- I'm full right now, so I don't have much of an ____. **(appetite)**
- Please put these ____ foods in the refrigerator. **(perishable)**

❸ Read each list of words and phrases. Ask students to supply the word that fits best with each.

- viewers, watchers, theatergoers **(audience)**
- stay away from, don't go near, try not to meet **(avoid)**
- can spoil or rot, should be refrigerated **(perishable)**
- hunger, desire to eat, liking of food **(appetite)**

❹ Read each sentence and ask students to decide if it is true or false. If the sentence is false, instruct students to explain why.

- Fruits are perishable. **(true)**
- If you don't have an appetite, you don't feel hungry. **(true)**
- A movie audience is a group of actors in a movie. **(false; the audience is the group of people who watch the movie)**
- When you avoid a friend, you try to find her. **(false; when you avoid a friend, you try to stay away from her)**

Answers for page 139: 1. B, 2. J, 3. B, 4. H

138

Name _____

Week 34
A Word a Day

Review Words perishable • appetite • audience • avoid

Fill in the bubble next to the correct answer.

1. What does an *audience* do?
   - Ⓐ performs on stage
   - Ⓑ watches a performance
   - Ⓒ cleans up an auditorium
   - Ⓓ sells snacks in a theater

2. Which of these is <u>not</u> *perishable*?
   - Ⓕ a loaf of bread
   - Ⓖ a bunch of carrots
   - Ⓗ a piece of meat
   - Ⓙ a stack of plates

3. When Jack *avoids* Jill, what does he do?
   - Ⓐ He goes over to Jill's house.
   - Ⓑ He leaves when he sees Jill coming.
   - Ⓒ He plays with Jill on the playground.
   - Ⓓ He brings Jill a nice birthday present.

4. When you have an *appetite* for a certain food, you ____.
   - Ⓕ do not like it at all
   - Ⓖ refuse to try it
   - Ⓗ feel hungry for it
   - Ⓙ know how to cook it

Writing

What would you do if you wanted to avoid being called on in class? Use **avoid** in your sentence.

_____

_____

© Evan-Moor Corp. • EMC 2792 • A Word a Day   139

Week 35
A Word a Day

blizzard

noun

A **blizzard** is a very heavy snowstorm.

After the **blizzard**, we had to dig our car out from under a pile of snow.

Which of these would you expect during a **blizzard**?

- ice on the windows
- freezing cold air
- bright sunshine
- a warm breeze
- a strong wind

If the weather forecast predicted a **blizzard**, what would you do to prepare for it?

disease

noun

A **disease** is a sickness or an illness.

I got a shot that will prevent me from getting a **disease** called measles.

Which of these are **diseases**?

- cancer
- freckles
- dimples
- chicken pox
- whooping cough

What do you and your family do to stay healthy in order to prevent getting **diseases**?

Week 35
A Word a Day

eager

adjective

If you're excited and can't wait to do something, you are **eager**.

> The **eager** children couldn't wait to get on the bus and go to the zoo.

Would you be **eager** if:
- you were going to the toy store?
- it was your day to do all the chores?
- it was time to open your birthday gifts?
- it was the first day of summer vacation?
- you had to go to bed an hour earlier than usual?

Tell about a time when you were **eager** to do something. How did you pass the time until it was time to do that activity?

enchanted

adjective

If something is **enchanted**, it has been put under a magic spell.

> The **enchanted** princess in the story slept for 100 years.

Which of the following might be **enchanted** in a fairy tale?
- a fairy
- a dragon
- a computer
- a talking frog
- a pair of socks

Tell about a favorite story or movie in which there was a character or thing that was **enchanted**. How did the person or thing become **enchanted**? Was the magic spell broken? How?

Review

Week 35
A Word a Day

blizzard • disease • eager • enchanted

Write on the board the four words studied this week. Read the words with the class and briefly review their meanings. Then conduct the oral activities below.

❶ Tell students that you are going to give them a clue about one of the words for the week. They are to find the word that answers the clue.

- This word could describe a frog that can speak English. **(enchanted)**
- You probably feel this way right before going on a trip with your family. **(eager to go)**
- Chicken pox is one. **(a disease)**
- This kind of storm is very snowy and windy. **(a blizzard)**

❷ Read each sentence and ask students to supply the correct word to complete the sentence.

- I was so ____ to go on vacation that I couldn't sleep. **(eager)**
- Mom won't drive in a ____ because it is dangerous. **(blizzard)**
- Cancer is a serious ____ that doctors can sometimes cure. **(disease)**
- In the ____ forest, the trees could walk and talk. **(enchanted)**

❸ Read each list of words and phrases. Ask students to supply the word that fits best with each.

- excited, enthusiastic, can't wait **(eager)**
- sickness, illness, infection **(disease)**
- snowy, windy, freezing cold **(blizzard)**
- magical, has a spell on, make-believe **(enchanted)**

❹ Read each sentence and ask students to decide if it is true or false. If the sentence is false, instruct students to explain why.

- Most people want to get a disease. **(false; a disease is an illness, which most people try to avoid getting)**
- Schools might close when a blizzard happens. **(true)**
- Enchanted creatures don't exist in real life. **(true)**
- When you're eager to see someone, you avoid him or her. **(false; when you're eager to see someone, you are excited to see that person)**

Answers for page 143: 1. C, 2. F, 3. D, 4. G

Name _____

Week 35
A Word a Day

Review Words blizzard • disease • eager • enchanted

Fill in the bubble next to the correct answer.

1. Which word has about the same meaning as *blizzard*?
   - Ⓐ desert
   - Ⓑ rainstorm
   - Ⓒ snowstorm
   - Ⓓ forest

2. Which might tell about *enchanted* creatures?
   - Ⓕ a fairy tale
   - Ⓖ a science book
   - Ⓗ a newspaper
   - Ⓙ a true story

3. Which word has about the same meaning as *disease*?
   - Ⓐ medicine
   - Ⓑ physician
   - Ⓒ hospital
   - Ⓓ sickness

4. When you are *eager* to go somewhere, you feel ___ about going.
   - Ⓕ unsure
   - Ⓖ enthusiastic
   - Ⓗ upset
   - Ⓙ okay, but not thrilled

Writing

Write about three things that you would be eager to do. Use **eager** in your sentence.

_____

_____

© Evan-Moor Corp. • EMC 2792 • A Word a Day

Week 36
A Word a Day

exhausted
adjective

When you are extremely tired, you're **exhausted**.

We were **exhausted** after hiking uphill all day long.

Would you be **exhausted** if you:
- ran a long race?
- went to bed early and slept late?
- worked at a school carwash all day?
- stayed up all night with a bad cough?
- sat on the porch reading and sipping lemonade?

Tell about a time when you felt **exhausted** and couldn't stay awake. What can you do to be sure you don't feel **exhausted** while you're in school?

frequent
adjective

If something happens often, it's **frequent**.

The **frequent** interruptions of the car alarm on the street made it hard to hear the teacher.

Which of these describe **frequent**?
- a lot
- once a year
- every ten years
- once every minute
- every five minutes

Tell about a time when you were trying to do something and had **frequent** interruptions. What happened? How did you feel?

Week 36
A Word a Day

halt

verb

When you **halt**, you come to a stop.

The police officer had the cars **halt** so that the man in the wheelchair could safely cross the street.

In which of these situations would you **halt**?

- at the park
- at a red light
- at a stop sign
- at a yellow light
- when you hear the siren of an emergency vehicle

Why is it important to **halt** when you come to a stop sign or a red light, or hear an emergency siren? What would happen if you didn't **halt**?

healthy

adjective

Someone or something that is in good physical condition is **healthy**.

It's important to get enough sleep if you want to stay **healthy**.

Which of the following are important things to do to stay **healthy**?

- eat junk food
- drink lots of water
- get plenty of exercise
- eat fruits and vegetables
- sit around watching television

What do you do to stay **healthy**? Describe some things that you eat and some of the ways you get exercise that help you stay **healthy**.

Review

Week 36
A Word a Day

exhausted • frequent • halt • healthy

Write on the board the four words studied this week. Read the words with the class and briefly review their meanings. Then conduct the oral activities below.

❶ Tell students that you are going to give them a clue about one of the words for the week. They are to find the word that answers the clue.

- To stay this way, people need to eat lots of fruits and vegetables. **(healthy)**
- This word would describe a thing that happens often. **(frequent)**
- Drivers do this when they come to stop signs. **(halt)**
- Hard work can make you feel this way. **(exhausted)**

❷ Read each sentence and ask students to supply the correct word to complete the sentence.

- My friend and I didn't get much sleep, so we felt ____ the next day. **(exhausted)**
- Getting plenty of exercise helps people to stay ____. **(healthy)**
- "____!" called the fire chief, and everyone stopped. **(Halt)**
- We take ____ trips to visit my grandma in Los Angeles. **(frequent)**

❸ Read each sentence and ask students to tell which word or words are wrong. Then have them provide the correct word from the week's list.

- I felt rested after getting very little sleep. **(rested/exhausted)**
- Eating less junk food will help you stay sick. **(sick/healthy)**
- "Keep going!" called the police officer, and everyone stopped. **(Keep going/Halt)**

❹ Read each sentence and ask students to decide if it is true or false. If the sentence is false, instruct students to explain why.

- Frequent events happen about once every five years. **(false; frequent events happen often)**
- Healthy people don't get sick very often. **(true)**
- If you were exhausted, you'd be eager to rest. **(true)**
- An army captain orders his soldiers to halt when he wants them to hurry up. **(false; he orders them to halt when he wants them to stop)**

Answers for page 147: 1. A, 2. H, 3. D, 4. H

Week 36
A Word a Day

Name _____

Review Words   exhausted • frequent • halt • healthy

Fill in the bubble next to the correct answer.

1. **Which word means the opposite of *halt*?**
   - Ⓐ start
   - Ⓑ speak
   - Ⓒ stand
   - Ⓓ sit

2. **When might someone feel *exhausted*?**
   - Ⓕ after nine or ten hours of sleep
   - Ⓖ after loafing around on the couch
   - Ⓗ after playing basketball for hours
   - Ⓙ after eating a good breakfast

3. **Which word has about the same meaning as *healthy*?**
   - Ⓐ sick
   - Ⓑ bored
   - Ⓒ excited
   - Ⓓ well

4. ***Frequent* family visits ___.**
   - Ⓕ never happen
   - Ⓖ happen about once a year
   - Ⓗ happen often
   - Ⓙ happen only in fairy tales

Writing

Write about a time when you felt exhausted but happy. Use **exhausted** in your sentence.

_____

_____

Dictionary

abandon • attempt

Aa

abandon • *verb*
When you abandon something, you leave it or give it up forever.
The pioneer family had to abandon its covered wagon when two of the wooden wheels broke.

abbreviated • *adjective*
A word that is written in a shortened form is abbreviated.
The abbreviated form of Texas is TX.

ability • *noun*
An ability is a skill or talent that you have.
Jill has the ability to hear a song and then play it on the piano.

accomplishment • *noun*
An accomplishment is something that has been done successfully.
It was a major accomplishment for the blind hiker to reach the top of the mountain peak.

advertise • *verb*
You advertise when you give information about something for sale.
My dad had to advertise in the paper for a week before he sold our old car.

affection • *noun*
When you show affection, you show feelings of love and caring.
Mai's puppy showed affection by licking her face.

agony • *noun*
If you're in agony, you're experiencing very strong pain.
I was in agony when I fell and broke my arm.

alert • *adjective*
When you're alert, you're wide-awake and able to act quickly.
A deer in the forest must be alert to protect itself from predators.

antics • *noun*
Antics are funny or silly actions.
We loved watching the clowns' antics when they squirted water at each other.

appetite • *noun*
Your appetite is your hunger for food.
I'm not allowed to have snacks after four o'clock so that I won't spoil my appetite for dinner.

artificial • *adjective*
Something artificial is not real or natural.
Dorthea's artificial nails looked real, but we knew they weren't.

assist • *verb*
When you help someone, you assist him or her.
The magician called for a volunteer from the audience to assist him with a trick.

attempt • *verb*
If you attempt something, you try to do it.
The juggler will attempt to juggle six flaming torches.

attire • *noun*

Your attire is the clothing you wear.

The proper attire for the banquet and dance is a suit or a gown.

audience • *noun*

An audience is a group of people who watch a show or a performance.

The audience clapped to let the actors know that they enjoyed the play.

available • *adjective*

If something is ready to be used, it is available.

My mom asked Jenny if she was available to baby-sit on Friday night.

avoid • *verb*

You avoid something if you try to stay away from it or keep it from happening.

Jenny avoided me at school because she borrowed my book and forgot to return it.

Bb

bargain • *noun*

A bargain is something that costs less than the usual price.

Aunt Emma saves lots of money by finding bargains at garage sales.

beverage • *noun*

A beverage is something to drink.

The Hawaiian restaurant was famous for its fruit beverages.

bizarre • *adjective*

Something that looks or acts odd or strange is bizarre.

The alien costume with three eyes and shiny scales was bizarre.

blizzard • *noun*

A blizzard is a very heavy snowstorm.

After the blizzard, we had to dig our car out from under a pile of snow.

brim • *noun*

The brim is the edge of a cup or bowl.

The tea spilled over the brim of the cup and into the saucer.

Cc

camouflage • *noun*

When colors and patterns are used to hide people, animals, or things, it is called camouflage.

When a chameleon changes color to blend into the environment, it uses camouflage.

ceremony • *noun*

A ceremony is an event held to mark a special occasion.

The graduation ceremony was held on the lawn outside the school.

chitchat • *verb*

When you chitchat, you talk about everyday, unimportant things.

My mom likes to chitchat on the phone with her sister about how her day went.

clench • *verb*

You clench something when you squeeze it tightly.

The baseball player clenched the bat as he stepped up to home plate.

clumsy • *adjective*

Someone or something that moves in an awkward, ungraceful way is clumsy.

I felt so clumsy when I tripped over my shoelace and dropped my lunch tray.

combine • *verb*

You combine things when you put two or more together.

You combine sugar, flour, butter, and eggs to make cookie dough.

companion • *noun*

A companion keeps someone company.

The guide dog was the blind woman's constant companion.

complicated • *adjective*

If something is complicated, it has lots of different parts or is difficult to understand.

My dad helped me follow the complicated directions for building my model car.

compromise • *verb*

When both sides give in a little to settle a disagreement, they compromise.

When Linda wanted to read and Janie wanted to watch a video, they compromised by listening to an audiobook.

consent • *noun*

Consent is permission to do something.

My parents have to give their written consent for me to go on a class field trip.

consequence • *noun*

A consequence is what happens as the result of another action.

One consequence of not doing homework might be getting a poor grade.

contagious • *adjective*

Something easily passed or spread to another person is contagious.

You're supposed to stay home from school if you have a contagious disease such as chicken pox.

convince • *verb*

You convince someone when you make him or her think the same way that you do.

I couldn't convince my mother to let me stay up late on a school night.

cozy • *adjective*

Something that feels warm, comfortable, and snug is cozy.

My cozy slippers keep my feet warm on cold winter nights.

Dd

dainty • *adjective*

Something is dainty when it is very delicate.

The dainty tea cakes crumbled when I dropped them.

decay • *verb*

When something decays, it becomes rotten.

If you don't want your teeth to decay, you need to brush them regularly.

definite • *adjective*

Something that is definite is certain or for sure.

My sister was definite about going to the movies, but I hadn't made up my mind.

dependable • *adjective*

Something or someone you can count on is dependable.

The guide dog was a dependable helper for the blind teenager.

detour • *noun*

A detour is a route you can follow when the main route is closed for some reason.

When the main road was being paved, we had to take a detour to get to our house.

disease • *noun*

A disease is a sickness or an illness.

I got a shot that will prevent me from getting a disease called measles.

disturb • *verb*

You disturb people when you bother, annoy, or interrupt them.

I wanted to read, so I hung a sign on my door that said "Do Not Disturb."

donate • *verb*

You donate when you give your time, money, or things to help others.

We will donate the money we earn from collecting cans to help feed homeless children.

doodle • *verb*

When you doodle, you draw or scribble while thinking about something else.

I like to doodle squiggly lines on bright paper when I'm listening to music.

dynamo • *noun*

A dynamo is an active person with lots of energy and enthusiasm.

Diana is a dynamo, performing in the school show, playing on a soccer team, and belonging to two clubs!

Ee

eager • *adjective*

If you're excited and can't wait to do something, you are eager.

The eager children couldn't wait to get on the bus and go to the zoo.

echo • *noun*

An echo is a sound that repeats because it bounces off a large surface.

After I yelled down to the hikers at the bottom of the canyon, the echo of my voice came back: "Hello . . . hello . . . hello . . ."

emotion • *noun*

An emotion is a feeling.

Actors must express every emotion, from sadness and disappointment to excitement and joy.

enchanted • forbid

enchanted • *adjective*

If something is enchanted, it has been put under a magic spell.

The enchanted princess in the story slept for 100 years.

enormous • *adjective*

If something is enormous, it's extremely large.

I thought bears were big, but the dinosaur at the museum was enormous!

enthusiastic • *adjective*

If you're really excited about something, you're enthusiastic about it.

The children were so enthusiastic about taking a vacation that they packed their suitcases a week early!

entire • *adjective*

The entire amount is all of it.

It's not a very good idea to eat an entire carton of ice cream for dessert.

errand • *noun*

An errand is a short trip to deliver or pick up something.

I went with my mom on her errands to the store, the library, and the gas station.

estimate • *verb*

When you estimate, you make a guess based on what you know.

There are too many jelly beans to count; let's try to estimate the number.

etiquette • *noun*

The rules of polite behavior, especially for social situations, are called etiquette.

It is good etiquette to chew with your mouth closed.

exchange • *verb*

When you exchange, you give something to someone and he or she also gives something to you.

We have a gift exchange in our club before the winter holidays.

exhausted • *adjective*

When you are extremely tired, you're exhausted.

We were exhausted after hiking uphill all day long.

Ff

famished • *adjective*

If you're famished, you are very, very hungry.

After I skipped lunch, I was so famished that I ate three helpings of everything at dinner.

flimsy • *adjective*

Something that is weak and lightweight is flimsy.

The weight of the books caused the flimsy box to break when I picked it up.

forbid • *verb*

When you forbid something, you tell someone they cannot do it.

Most parents forbid their children to eat sweets right before dinner.

frequent • *adjective*

If something happens often, it's frequent.

The frequent interruptions of the car alarm on the street made it hard to hear the teacher.

furious • *adjective*

If you are furious, you're extremely angry.

My mom was furious when our dog dug up her favorite rosebush.

Gg

generous • *adjective*

A person who is willing to share with others is generous.

The generous man shared his prize money with his friends.

gleam • *verb*

When something gleams, it shines and gives off or reflects light.

The medal hanging around the winner's neck gleamed in the sunlight.

grant • *verb*

When you grant something to a person, you allow him or her to have it.

The fairy waved her magic wand and said, "I will grant you one wish."

grip • *verb*

When you hold something very tightly, you grip it.

The climber gripped the rope as she made her way up the steep mountain.

grumble • *verb*

When you grumble, you complain in a grumpy way.

My brother always grumbles when Mom reminds him to do his chores.

Hh

habit • *noun*

A habit is the usual way you act or do things.

Doing your homework at the same time every day is a good habit to get into!

halt • *verb*

When you halt, you come to a stop.

The police officer had the cars halt so that the man in the wheelchair could safely cross the street.

hardy • *adjective*

When something is hardy, it can survive in difficult conditions.

The hardy cactus can survive in the blistering desert sun.

harmless • *adjective*

Something is harmless if it's safe and causes no harm or injury.

We thought the snake was poisonous, but it turned out to be harmless.

harmony • *noun*

If you work in complete cooperation with others, you work in harmony.

The ballplayers worked in such harmony that they easily won the game.

healthy • *adjective*

Someone or something that is in good physical condition is healthy.

It's important to get enough sleep if you want to stay healthy.

hideous • *adjective*

Something hideous is ugly or horrible to look at.

The monster in the movie was so hideous that I had to close my eyes.

hodgepodge • *noun*

A hodgepodge is a disorderly, jumbled mess of things.

Jimmy could not find his truck in the hodgepodge of toys on the floor.

huddle • *verb*

When a group of people or animals crowd together, they huddle.

The whole family tried to huddle under one umbrella when they were caught in the rain.

hue • *noun*

A hue is a color or a shade of a color.

I couldn't decide whether to color the flower a light or dark red hue.

humorous • *adjective*

Something funny or amusing is humorous.

The cartoon he brought in was so humorous that we all laughed.

hustle • *verb*

If you hustle, you move very quickly and with lots of energy.

We really have to hustle if we want to catch the movie that starts in ten minutes.

Ii

ideal • *adjective*

Something that is just perfect is ideal.

Our timing was ideal. The bus arrived just as we got to the bus stop!

identical • *adjective*

When things are exactly alike, they're identical.

The twins were identical. You could not tell one from the other.

imitate • *verb*

You imitate when you copy something or someone.

Grace tried to imitate her sister by dressing like her.

infant • *noun*

An infant is a baby.

The infant was sleeping peacefully in her crib.

ingredients • *noun*

Ingredients are what you put together to make something else.

Rick put all the ingredients for the cookies into the bowl, and I stirred them.

inhabit • *verb*

You inhabit the place where you live.

Bats inhabit the caves on this cliff.

inquire • nominate

inquire • *verb*

When you inquire, you try to find out something by asking a question.

For information on when the movie begins, you can inquire at the ticket window.

interview • *verb*

You interview someone when you meet and ask questions in order to find out about the person.

The sports reporter was eager to interview the players on the winning team.

Jj

jiffy • *noun*

A jiffy is a very short amount of time.

When the runner's shoe came untied in the middle of the race, she tied it in a jiffy.

journey • *noun*

A journey is a long trip or an adventure.

The journey across the Great Plains in covered wagons took a long time.

jovial • *adjective*

A jovial person is always laughing and in a good mood.

Our jovial neighbor always has a funny joke or silly trick for us.

Ll

lagoon • *noun*

A lagoon is a small area of shallow water near a larger body of water.

Water from the ocean reached the lagoon at high tide.

loaf • *verb*

You loaf when you spend time being lazy and doing nothing.

I would rather loaf on the weekend than do my chores and yardwork.

Mm

miniature • *adjective*

Something miniature is smaller than its usual size.

The miniature cars in my collection look just like real ones.

modern • *adjective*

Something that is from recent times is modern.

Modern refrigerators use much less energy than older ones.

monotone • *noun*

When you speak in a monotone, you don't use any expression in your voice.

The speaker's monotone almost put the audience to sleep.

Nn

nominate • *verb*

You nominate someone when you suggest that he or she would be right for a job or deserves special recognition.

I want to nominate Henry to head the party committee because he has lots of good ideas.

Oo

obnoxious • *adjective*

When something is disagreeable and unpleasant, it is obnoxious.

The play was ruined by some obnoxious people in the audience who were talking during the show.

occupation • *noun*

An occupation is a person's job or career.

A firefighter has an exciting and dangerous occupation.

occupy • *verb*

You occupy a place when you live in it.

We can occupy the house just as soon as they finish painting it.

omit • *verb*

When you omit something, you leave it out.

If you omit your name on your book report, your teacher won't know whose it is.

opinion • *noun*

Your opinion is what you think about something.

I thought the movie would be exciting, but I changed my opinion after I saw it.

original • *adjective*

Something is original if it is the first of its kind.

The inventor became famous for all his original ideas for new machines.

Pp

participate • *verb*

When you take part in something, you participate.

She didn't want to participate in the game, so she just watched.

passenger • *noun*

A passenger rides in a vehicle driven or piloted by another person.

The pilot had to park the plane before the passengers could unbuckle their seat belts.

pastry • *noun*

A sweet baked good made from dough is called a pastry.

The bakery smelled delicious early in the morning after the pastries were baked.

perishable • *adjective*

Something that can spoil or rot is perishable.

Because meat is perishable, we keep it in the cooler when we go camping.

physician • *noun*

A physician is a doctor.

The physician checked my throat, and then he wrote a prescription for some medicine.

portion • *noun*

A portion is a part or a share of something.

I ate only one piece of pie, but my brother had two portions.

pounce • *verb*

You pounce when you jump on something suddenly.

The deer got away before the crouching mountain lion could pounce on it.

predict • *verb*

When you predict, you say what you think will happen in the future.

Weather forecasters use computers to help them predict the weather.

prevent • *verb*

If you keep something from happening, you prevent it.

We can prevent some diseases by giving people vaccinations.

putrid • *adjective*

If something is putrid, it is rotten and smells awful.

After sitting in the sun for two days, the garbage was putrid.

Qq

queasy • *adjective*

If you feel sick to your stomach, you feel queasy.

The rolling of the boat during the storm made everyone feel queasy.

Rr

rambunctious • *adjective*

When you act wild and noisy, you are being rambunctious.

The children were being so rambunctious that the librarian asked them to go outside.

recite • *verb*

If you recite something, you say it aloud from memory.

Our class learned a poem by heart to recite at the school assembly.

refuse • *verb*

If you say no to something, you refuse it.

When Martin was asked to baby-sit, he refused because he had made other plans.

retrieve • *verb*

When you get something back, you retrieve it.

I had to retrieve my homework from the trash after I threw it away by mistake.

Ss

scarce • *adjective*

Something is scarce if it's hard to get or find.

Parking spaces were scarce at the mall on the day of the big sale.

scholar • *noun*

A scholar is a person who has studied and learned a lot.

Professor Rossi, a famous music scholar, knows about all kinds of music.

shelter • *noun*

A shelter is a safe place to stay.

When it started raining, we found shelter in a nearby store to keep dry.

shipshape • tremble

shipshape • *adjective*
If something is clean, neat, and in order, it's shipshape.
I don't get my weekly allowance until my room is shipshape.

shriek • *verb*
When you shriek, you let out a loud, high-pitched scream.
When my mom saw that mouse, she let out a shriek that scared even me!

slither • *verb*
When something slithers, it moves with a gliding motion.
We watched the snake slither on its belly up and over the rock.

spectator • *noun*
A spectator is a person who watches an event without participating in it.
I usually like to play basketball, but today I'm going to be a spectator in the stands.

sturdy • *adjective*
Something sturdy is strong and solid.
The sturdy bookshelf was able to hold the weight of many books.

swarm • *noun*
A swarm is a large number of insects, animals, or people that move together as a group.
We had to stay inside because a swarm of bees had just left its hive.

Tt

talented • *adjective*
When you have a natural ability to do something well, you are talented.
The talented young singer sang as well as a professional recording artist.

tedious • *adjective*
If something is tedious, it is boring and repetitious.
We thought that writing all of our spelling words ten times was tedious.

tempting • *adjective*
Something that's inviting and hard to resist is tempting.
Although I had work to do, his offer to go to the beach was too tempting to pass up.

tidy • *adjective*
A tidy place is very neat, with everything in order.
Her room was so tidy that she could always find anything she needed.

topple • *verb*
When something topples, it falls over.
The tree was about to topple over in the strong wind.

tremble • *verb*
When you tremble, you shake with fear, excitement, or cold.
I was so nervous before the race, I started to tremble.

trio • *noun*

A trio is a group of three.

The three girls called their singing trio "Wee Three."

trivial • *adjective*

When something is trivial, it has little importance.

Your book report doesn't need to mention the number of illustrations in the story. That's trivial information.

Uu

unusual • *adjective*

If something is strange or different, it's unusual.

It was unusual for my dad to be home at three o'clock in the afternoon instead of around dinnertime.

Vv

vacant • *adjective*

When a place is empty, it is vacant.

The vacant house will be painted before new people move in.

variety • *noun*

There is variety when there are many different items to choose from.

My mom buys a package with a variety of small cereal boxes so that I can eat a different cereal every day.

vigorous • *adjective*

When something is vigorous, it is strong, active, and full of energy.

Vigorous exercise makes your heart work harder.

villain • *noun*

The villain is an evil or wicked character in a story, movie, or play.

In old cowboy movies, the villain usually wears black, and the hero usually wears white.

volume • *noun*

The loudness of a sound or noise is its volume.

We always turn down the volume on the TV when someone is on the phone.

Ww

warning • *noun*

A warning is a message that alerts you to danger or to a bad thing that might happen.

We left the building when the fire alarm gave us a loud warning.

wince • *verb*

You wince when you pull back or make a face in fear, pain, or dislike.

I wince every time my pet snake eats a mouse.

Zz

zany • *adjective*

A person who acts zany behaves in a foolish or silly way.

The zany clown was honking a giant horn and squirting water from a flower on his coat.

Index

abandon	92	dainty	4
abbreviated	52	decay	48
ability	20	definite	88
accomplishment	120	dependable	80
advertise	64	detour	133
affection	44	disease	140
agony	73	disturb	36
alert	41	donate	117
antics	108	doodle	101
appetite	136	dynamo	21
artificial	97	eager	141
assist	129	echo	17
attempt	81	emotion	53
attire	9	enchanted	141
audience	137	enormous	104
available	112	enthusiastic	132
avoid	137	entire	124
bargain	52	errand	100
beverage	132	estimate	113
bizarre	37	etiquette	33
blizzard	140	exchange	96
brim	13	exhausted	144
camouflage	24	famished	77
ceremony	88	flimsy	28
chitchat	73	forbid	84
clench	8	frequent	144
clumsy	116	furious	100
combine	92	generous	5
companion	37	gleam	56
complicated	69	grant	28
compromise	25	grip	49
...sent	76	grumble	13
...quence	125	habit	93
...ous	97	halt	145
	65	hardy	53
	113	harmless	93

harmony	56	portion	84
healthy	145	pounce	4
hideous	68	predict	72
hodgepodge	41	prevent	112
huddle	85	putrid	17
hue	24	queasy	61
humorous	125	rambunctious	5
hustle	77	recite	105
ideal	57	refuse	121
identical	45	retrieve	40
imitate	108	scarce	44
infant	20	scholar	32
ingredients	89	shelter	116
inhabit	45	shipshape	72
inquire	8	shriek	104
interview	65	slither	128
jiffy	124	spectator	12
journey	81	sturdy	128
jovial	57	swarm	117
lagoon	109	talented	29
loaf	60	tedious	64
miniature	36	tempting	120
modern	49	tidy	133
monotone	9	topple	16
nominate	60	tremble	68
obnoxious	32	trio	40
occupation	76	trivial	21
occupy	61	unusual	121
omit	2	vacant	85
opinion	29	variety	101
original	109	vigorous	33
participate	48	villain	80
passenger	89	volume	69
pastry	105	warning	96
perishable	136	wince	25
physician	129	zany	16

A Word a Day • EMC 2792 • © Evan-Moor Corp.